Also by Brenda Hillman

POETRY

White Dress

Fortress

Death Tractates

Bright Existence

Loose Sugar

Cascadia

Pieces of Air in the Epic

Practical Water

Seasonal Works with Letters on Fire

CHAPBOOKS

Coffee, 3 A.M.

Autumn Sojourn

The Firecage

Four Poets (with Brett Fletcher Lauer, Joshua Marie Wilkinson, and
    Andrew Zawacki)

Her Presence Will Live Beyond Progress

AS EDITOR

The Poems of Emily Dickinson

The Grand Permission: New Writings on Poetics and Motherhood
    (with Patricia Dienstfrey)

Writing the Silences: Selected Poems of Richard O. Moore (with Paul Ebenkamp)

Particulars of Place by Richard O. Moore (with Garrett Caples and Paul Ebenkamp)

AS TRANSLATOR

Instances by Jeonrye Choi (with the author and Wayne de Fremery)

Poems from Above the Hill: Selected Poems of Ashur Etwebi (with the author
    and Diallah Haidar)

At Your Feet by Ana Cristina Cesar (with Helen Hillman and Sebastião Macedo)

Extra
Hidden
Life,
among
the
Days

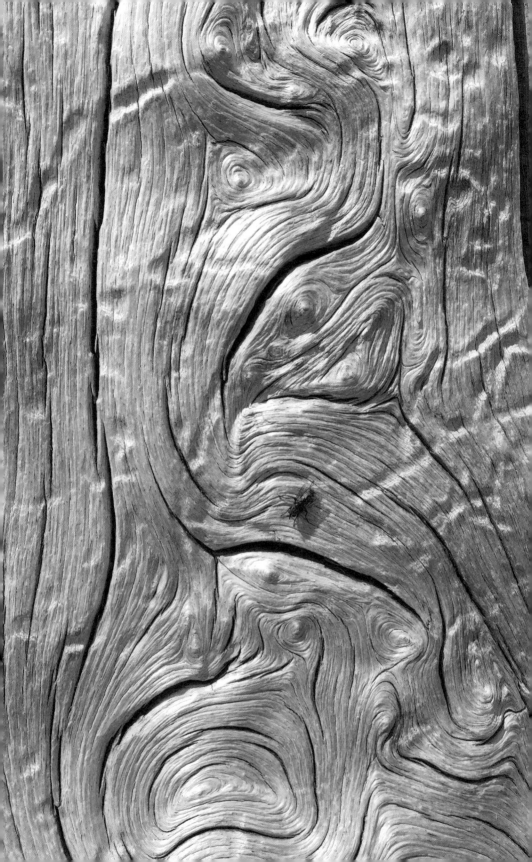

**Brenda
Hillman**

Extra
Hidden
Life,
among
the
Days

**Wesleyan
University
Press**
Middletown,
Connecticut

Wesleyan Poetry

Wesleyan University Press

Middletown CT 06459

www.wesleyan.edu/wespress

© 2018 Brenda Hillman

All rights reserved

Manufactured in the United States of America

Library of Congress Cataloging-in-Publication Data

Names: Hillman, Brenda, author.

Title: Extra hidden life, among the days / Brenda Hillman.

Description: Middletown, Connecticut : Wesleyan University Press, [2018]

Series: Wesleyan poetry | Includes bibliographical references.

Identifiers: LCCN 2017036431 | ISBN 9780819578051 (cloth : alk. paper)

Classification: LCC PS3558.I4526 A6 2018 | DDC 811/.54—dc23

LC record available at https://lccn.loc.gov/2017036431

Designed by Quemadura

5 4 3 2 1

Contents

I. The Forests of Grief & Color

Perhaps grief is imagined to end in violence, as if grief itself could be killed. Can we perhaps find one of the sources of nonviolence in the capacity to grieve, to stay with the unbearable loss without converting it into destruction? If we could bear our grief, would we be less inclined to strike back or strike out? And if the grief is unbearable, is there another way to live with it that is not the same as bearing it?

Judith Butler, "On Grief and Rage"

This mycorrhizal network architecture suggests an efficient and robust network, where large trees play a foundational role in facilitating conspecific regeneration and stabilizing the ecosystem.

"Architecture of the wood-wide web: Rhizopogon spp. genets link multiple Douglas-fir cohorts" http://onlinelibrary.wiley.com/doi/10.1111/j.1469-8137.2009.03069.x/full

. . . I will open my dark saying upon the harp.

Psalm 49

On a Day, In the World

We had a grief
we didn't understand while
standing at the edge of
some low scrub hills as if
humans were extra
or already gone;–

what had been in us before?
a life that asks for mostly
wanting freedom to get things done
in order to feel less
helpless about the end
of things alone–;

when i think of time on earth,
i feel the angle of gray minutes
entering the medium days
yet not "built-up":: our
work together: groups, the willing
burden of an old belief,

& beyond them love, as of
a great life going like fast
creatures peeling back marked
seeds, gold-brown integuments
the color time
will be when we are gone–

Whose Woods These Are We Think

(ekphrastic haibun)

When they ask "What are you working on now that the elements are finished" i say the elements are never finished; in China they have metal, in India they have ether, in the West we are short on time. Wood has also been named as an element. In white Euro fairy tales, children are sent into the woods, probably the Black Forest, carrying baskets covered with cloth made by child laborers just as factories are beginning. When i first read the Frost snowy woods piece as a desert child in the 60s, i experienced a calm as he enters the whose woods these are he thinks he knows, though i didn't know that many woods in Tucson or a little horse thinking it queer or a village. What would it have been like to be sent out with a small covered basket if you were a peasant child into what we now call the ecotone, the region between two environments– a marsh with striped frogs for example– then on into the woods where a peasant uprising is being planned.

> We have sent them all into the woods
>
> We have sent them all into the woods
>
> We have sent them all into the woods

& we know exactly whose thin logged-out woods these are. What do people need from poetry during the changes? The changes are immeasurable. Perception, form, & material locked into the invisible. Many need calm poetry, especially at weddings where they feel uneasy, & i would certainly write that way if i believed calm were key to any of it, but if what woods are left are lovely, dark, deep, they are also oblique, obscure, magical, owned for profit, full of fragile unnamed species, scarce on time, time that barely exists though people base their lives on imagining it does. i hoped to find some wisdom to send back to you & that is what i am working on now, my present hopeful wild & unknown friends . . .

All-night Crooked Moonrise
over Mountain Pines

Scraping, on the horizon–   & the disk

rose, throbbing, to the triple cloud–

the enigma responded: in the forest,

a wood mind swayed on the crest
while the angle brought ground water,
  always a thin other, down
              to the river . . .   Through lace life, late life
  light rises bent /// – you stand a while;

& if, at midnight, that raw moon

slashes your bed

through the cage of the blinds,

oh now the sweet owl
calls to its cripple
      & hurries across the meadow

where *t i m e* is carried, tranquil & stretched
            — how can knowledge spread itself *thus*,
unable to sort itself out?   & you might weather this:

you feared no one would love you
& when they did, you feared
you would not be forgiven

such a small word, *time*
yet it is friends
with both nothings–

The Bride Tree Can't Be Read

The bride tree puts down its roots
below the phyla. It is there
when we die & when we are born,
middle & upper branches reaching
the planet heart by the billions
during a revolution we don't see.

Quarks & leptons are cooling
on their infant stems, spinning the spinning
brain of matter, fled to electrical dark
water, species with names the tree
can hold in the shale shade brought
by the ambulance of art;

no one but you knows what occurred
in the dress you wore in the dream
of atonement, the displaced tree in
the dream you wore, a suffering endurable
only once, edges that sought release
from envy to a more endurable loss,

a form to be walked past, that has
outworn the shame of time,
its colors sprung through description
above a blaze of rhizomes spreading
in an arable mat that mostly
isn't simple but is calm & free—

Brief Walk at Salt Point Park

–seal pups   *ar-ar-ar-* –

& the skin of the soul felt a chill,
        especially the left side   of the
S, facing the Pacific (specific   Pacific
            specific Pacific   *ar ar ar*);

sandstock   burdock   human   s   pines

(does the *s* move toward *pines* or *spines*?)

– buckwheat   hardpan   up a hill
finding   the rim of the miracle–

    fear   blue   shade   sense
      blind   made   what   tense
        pigmy cypress   trill   or   hill

(knowledge did not wreck   experience–)

weather warped   & nations fell
    over the edge of the miracle–

–What thus doth keep love safe, brittle rhymer
–Depends on what you mean by safe, *little climber*

(To know without fear the mind of another)

For the Lovers
Abandoned in Sunlight

Some friends had broken up–;
i didn't think they should,
but still... (The bees had also
flown away to the chrome woods–
    maybe the workers went ahead, but how?
    No one understood–) The lovers
    lifted yeses   then a no . . .
    Why? (*let's not get into*
a whole thing about it . . .) Their hours never
    snagged despair;   why could they
not have loved each other more?

One day the hive returned,
like a gold thought in the gray
context of an oversight . . .
    the lovers would find others
all too soon with basic need less
    passionate than the first;   i went on
    with my reading & the bees worked
right up to the finished dusk
        as if their house
            would stay near mine in a drought-
tested thicket remote in time–

During a Suite by Gaspar Cassadó

Transfixed   by the bow

only simply above: sighs of wood

& horsehair breath of the cello,
   your azure perceptions /// . . .

(does *it* perceive also?)

as if pierced by   *saudades*!

This night   far from your pain tangled
   with frog song

(such distance to the next town)

& your suffering   cannot be measured—
não a luar

in this universal background—

Beneath a Dying Coast Live Oak

–to have made the mistake
of not caring –for one day! –
   you stood in the parking lot . . .
   where, on the ground: globe
of the wasp gall   (the pupae
cannot peek out
through tiny Garamond ellipsis dots
of the outer shell . . .)
   when suddenly, above:
         grrr rrrrr gimme gimme gimme
         squirrels trying to mate
         in the oak, the dire twain
            of their warring tails . . .
(sex is so much trouble outdoors!)

   –the fear the loved ones
would end up alone
since humans will not modify
   desire, & nothing
      comes together anymore–
      democracy & time,
from *da*: to divide–
      there was the love you could not
      live without, & you
had lost it, though you stood
            inside the life
            that gave you life–

[& heard a humming, like the]

—& heard a humming, like the
start of time . . .
  & when the wind agreed,
      the knobs of song molecules fit into
    the frog,   a knowledge heard
the humming, without fear—
  (puffball, spinning, among
    the dimensions: –
      wears itself out,
      wears itself out, by evening . . .)
to know,   *what*, in a day?
      to have thought
the children safe,   & the little woods–
  that thought must be given back . . .

      not safe, & lost – you could
    text but they might not text back . . .
    Not to be *undone* by this.
(even if?) even if.
(even if?) even if.
        . . . to rest
with what must be given up: there was
      a breaking at the start of time,
    then love that
broke the breaking . . .

The Forests of Grief & Color

        –Listening,
          past the hazel bank. . . . the changed life
      lies under, prior
    to purr–; new species grow
      cold spores, inside
casing strewn . . .   Groups & nations
      howl unseen . . .   The mind
      god-labors
         pumping itself green. It's
then your true eye
        gathers   its half
loves;   pollen floats
  upstream in doubt,
    in the shadow   of a drought;
  (put the phone down,
you're just about
out of opposites,   oh,
    dark evening–   sink . . .)

   In brief
    woods, there's lignan
  at work,   past profit,
such comfort to decay,   wood
  mind would,   so small
to say: "apart, fled" –!
  Hold in hope, not . . . *out*! not to go
    out among them,   yet . . .
    (to have important work
among the dead–)

The Before Sleep Kind of Everything

(What is the edge of the self–?)
      (The edge of the self
  is the *f*,   its awning of breath–)
    The old woman greets death
in her bed   – – the peril cloud
ascends – "well done!"
   She dozes off   & feels for those
   she cannot help but feel fear for –;

    Over the ledge
   of sound – Vast sage!
It visits her,
     she must sleep widely then. – And
   when the mild dead hover . . .   she clings
clings   clings to the rim
    of the prayer wheel –   Now

    motion goes on   to release her –;
she   helped you   unknow
the half-true –.
     After, she greets the greeters . . .
   radiant roots,   reluctantly brought:
beside the creamy chaos   of the stars –

Composition: Fringe Lichen: Tilde & Mãe

As i have since i was a child in summer, found a rock with a fine example
of life;

this time *Flavopunctelia soredica,* fringe lichen, with tilde-like edges;

to extend a sound where other life could hear,

in hopes of accomplishing nothing, offered punctuation to the lichen, to
my mother who was very quiet at the time

so it would be heard & not heard in the heavenly sphere, at least, as the
brain imagined it there, making absolute motion, in a harmless frame, as
the granite has spoken since i was a child, in other words,

i said *mãe*

with 10 rows of 12 tildes & 2 rows of *mãe,* in Portuguese,
i recited the tildes by lifting a finger, recited the "mãe" lines,
tapping toward where she lives very quietly in days she creates . . .

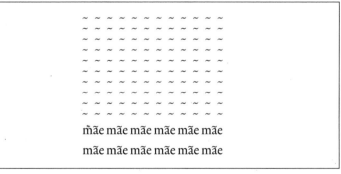

Composition: Under Cypresses, Near Big Sur

Before bronze winter, unable to get good sorrow through,

choosing a rock where a *Xanthoparmelia* shield had spread,

facing the full-of-plastic Pacific, eager to include crows,

waiting for one crow to disrupt the cantata of not-crow,

counting by thinking, as for decades, i've thought punctuation has
features of skylight, *tsk-ing*,

(my brothers used to say *tsk tsk*, when we were naughty),

hoping this might lift the dread of being human, & early, relieved by dots
in the air,

i repeated a composition 6 times with the crow & tried to breathe
humanly, thus:

```
: : : : : : aw  aw  aw : : :

: : : : : : aw  aw  aw : : :

: : : : : : aw  aw  aw : : :

: : : : : : aw  aw  aw : : :

: : : : : : aw  aw  aw : : :

: : : : : : aw  aw  aw : : :
```

(for M.W.)

Of Monarchs Again,
Especially the Stripes

—or, perhaps we could
care less carefully now . . .
              that they fluttered
   in the forest, with mid-
gold clinging to their going . . . Their cadence
         became   our anxiety:
night vision, to rest as a speckled   gleam,
an ochre glance.   The days can sometimes
            give them
         what they need–that's
         pretty obvious (triangles of
orange– a weight had been dispatched–)
we're visitors, & only briefly, at that,

      —one more flutter
   from the spirit world, glittering
time looks on, souls
         as seeds, ready to rise, & stay . . .
as if color has chosen to live,
            no matter what
            (it both is &
            isn't a metaphor–)

                                        for KH

So, Bacteria Also Have Their Thunder

           & cloud caps
     in the drought–   microbes in my gut &
on the leg of the bobcat,   microbes even
      on its photo–, buckles near
grasses of perhaps not growing . . .
no rain this week,   no relief sounds . . . in our grief
here, to hear coastal cypress– beware–
    so grown things rain:
between life & nonlife &
     death: the whir
under the dove's wing, to – rows of marigolds,

    an end of earth where creatures go
without supervision . . . such
      sorrow i heard–
  such sorrow they heard . . . bacteria
also have their thunder   in the nightlight
  of the biome, coasting,
     outside an arrogant noise
they never made – breaks
  energy in   sun's
     setting   behind a band
of   thunder clouds: cracks & volunteers–

Angrily Standing
Outside in the Wind

–kept losing *self control*
but how could one lose the self
after reading so much literary theory?
The shorter "i" stood under the cork trees,
   the taller "I" remained rather passive;
the brendas were angry at the greed, angry
that the trees would die, had lost interest
in the posturing of the privileged,

  the gaps between can't & won't . . .
Stood outside the gate of permissible
   sound & the wind came *soughing*
through the doubt debris
(*soughing* comes from *swāgh*–to resound . . .
echo actually comes from this also–)
  we thought of old Hegel across
the sea– the *Weltgeist*–& clouds

went by like the bones of a Kleenex . . .
   it's too late for countries
but it's not too late for trees . . .
   & the wind kept *soughing*
  with its sound sash, wind with
   its sound sash, increasing
bold wind with its sound sash,
   increasing bold–

[Untitled Day]

In the dream, they were doing better,
    i could see that. He had
 bought a suit; they could
    laugh together (though not always
at the same things);
     & where they sat–
    a glow (from
 the window ledge,

    lined with small
   recent jars,   in fringe-training–)
brought in the common day–
   filled not with wisdom
    but with insights & their variants–;
when you send in your request
   you have to know what
    you are working with . . .

i said to the dream, take
  this ordeal . . . (what's good
for the night is never
   a belief . . .–) The room
    was the gold of five
  days in summer
though the chairs were made of wood
  from the forest of grief–

Species Prepare to
Exist after Money

Turns out bacteria communicate in color.
   They warn each other in teal
  or celadon & humans assign
meaning to this, saying they are distressed
   or full of longing. The wood rat
  makes a nest of H's; it hoards
the seven tiny silences. Crows in the pine
can count specific faces like writers
   who feel their art has been ignored.
        My father spent his life thinking
     about money though he knew
    it causes most of this stupid violence,

  & he thought of me as a sensible person;
     you have the chemical for sensible, he said.
There was no tragedy between us,
        unlike how poor Joyce wrote
    that his daughter turned away
from *that battered cabman's face, the world.*
    i didn't turn away because i don't know
where it is, it is all over, & when it seems
    pure nothingness has come to pass,
i know another animal prepares itself
    nationless, not sensible;
       thinking of it helps a little bit–

Extra Hidden Life, among the Days

Sometimes , when i'm
very tired ,   i think
of extremophiles   ,   chemolithoautotrophs
& others with   power for changing
not-life into lives ,   of those that eat rock
& fire in volcanoes   ,   before the death
of the world but after   the death of a human
, of their taste
for ammonia or iron   ,   sulfur & carbon
, somehow
enough of it to go on . . . As workers
taste revolt   ,   they grow
at the vents of oceans ,   turning mute vapor
into respiration   ,   changing unhinged
matter to hinges   ,   near the rims of sea
trenches or the caves . . .   Our friend wrote
of writers living   in gray hiding,
, of those who love glass
& early freedom ,   steep sand
& late freedom   ,   sex among gentle
or bitter grasses   ,   those with a taste for
blue or belligerence ,   *obscure lives,* she
called them   ,   the writers
of radical mind   . . .
The living prefer life   ,   mostly they do
, they are ravenous
, making shapes in groups
as the dying grow   one thought

until the end ,   wanting more
specifics ,   *desert* or *delay*
until the i   drops away into
i am not here ,   the mineral other
pumps & vast vapors ,   ridges & shadows beyond
the single life it had not thought of–

for CDW

Mountain Pond Landscape, in a Drought

—Gotten the black, the tally,
finished the seeds,
            the breath . . . Rattle
    behind the sun, not ready:
fern friend: fern frond. Aster for mourning
    the water, not ready.
                        Down talus fir tree
coppery each (sounds like
coppery beech) flattish needle
        attached with a scar . . .
            ssswhite seeds fall up . . .
        daughter daylight proud
of itself–; we pleased
                our fathers mildly enough.
ough. slough. slough. slew . . .   Word
skins float by;
the word *word* is such
    a strange word!– from *wer*[*[*schwa*]*], to speak–
        far fewer words be spoken now . . .
Beardtongue, fleabane, swallowed
    a slip & you, human, making
        blunt appeal to syllables
                with flesh, mosquitoes
looking for blood,   our liquid trick–

As a Sentence Leaves Its Breath

—on a mountain top in summer
wood splitting on a finished tree, —
ridges of the swirls in a mirrorless day,
tall ants nearby–, twin sides of alive: so pattern recalls
how to cling volute, contingent,
as the dying breath could cling, obstinate, to texture,
needing more information, or if the sentence,
swings on the imperfect hearer, risking leaving
the close days without fear–;
as the sentence leaves its breath, in the warmth
no matter what: things you said about the things
you said, wanting the written life, a phrase striving

for nothing spoken among the rats & hawks
& spirits on the hill, the spiral ear of wind,
in the space of the circular where sounds go,
impossible, intense, inner– existence
loved more in the common zones, brief
stop in each, as one man prays not terrible prayers,
silences to each, an act to prefer;
so the sentence leaves the word,
clinging to a group of dawns– a swirl on wood
reaching in the air–this unlikely thought,
to know or stay, to say so long,
infinite home:– now you must be everyone–

for FG

Some Kinds of Forever Visit You

The unknowns are up early;
they browse through the bronze
porch bells. Crows
call & late
apples blaze
toward western emptiness.
In your illness,
the edges hesitate;
like the revolt
of workers, they
will take a while . . .

Here comes the fond
mild winter; other
realms are noisy
& unanimous. You tap
the screen & dream
while waiting; four
kinds of forever
visit you today:
something, nothing,
everything & art,
greater than you are
& of your making–

for AS

The Bride Tree Lives Three Times

In willing textures where the wood rat lives
   the drought lets trees die twice.
   Realism & magic steady one another
  & the hurt in your heart
     from the human fact
circles the edge of the park. The bride
   tree blooms late this year, its nature
   stored at the edge of day–

 some like to avoid the word *nature*
but what to put in its place
   for ants & thoughts & parking meters,
stars & skin & granite, quarks,
   the world above & below . . .
When you are confused about poetry
& misunderstand its brown math,
   the sessile branches & a seal of awe

attach the tree to the dark.
   Someday, you'll need less evidence;
the missing won't cease to exist.
For now, you stop to eat the free fruit
   only you knew would appear
& for that, you have your human hands,
  infinite nature, a single
   body standing on this earth–

In the Forest of Blue Aptitude

At the edge of winter, when
the wood-rat hides for its first
repose & the invisible is thick,
        old meanings can always be
brought through; the owl sleeps
longer than its prey & you recall

where you were a child
& words were seen in nimble
magic they themselves proposed.
        Later, in failed communities
of law, they gave almost
no advice & now you continue

that service on your own, where
    secrets meet contours as your
philosopher supposed, in abstract
shadows tossed over a sheaf
    of news retreating from events.
So, how should meaning find you?

It is a glow in the cloth. As if a row
    of children carried lanterns unopposed
        through a forest of blue aptitude:
they looked like you. What they feared
most had never arrived. What they
    loved most was already here.

for BBH

II.
Near the
Rim of
the Ideal

for **Amiri Baraka**
for **Geoffrey G. O'Brien**

Arrests are increasing daily, but other than that, everything is quite cheerful.
   Róża Luxemburg, letter to Luise & Karl Kautsky, January 2, 1906

History was like that for a while.
   Michael Palmer, *Alogon*

A Short Rhyme for Amiri Baraka

A hawk skims the exterior
of the interior hill–   piercing non-syllables
you cannot dream–;   its sound is extreme,
red rick-rack on a hill,   red's arid
shadow on the other side,
chattering with dead men in dead books,
shattering with red men in red nooks,
no more anger than he's
supposed to do, but
angry enough, check-check-check,
not angry enough to not to,   & who
are we to judge at the edges, & where,
who throw money at death
who throw money at death
who throw money at death
who throw money at death
who throw money at death
who throw money at death

A Summer Song
From Old Berlin

i   plucked   a   little
leaf   from   Hegel's   grave;
it   glowed   from   scallops
in   a   coat   of
arms,   &   silence   was
one   of   its   features–;
in   nearby   Europe,   they
are   storming   the   palace;
lindens   wait   like   history–;
we   were   calmer   when
we   were   there,   reading
in   the   grander   glare,
reading   dates   by   old
canals   in   pewter   light,
the   myth   of   living
more   than   once,   as
Hegel   thought   (&   thought)
like   that   creature   under
a   waterfall,   the   one
with   the   jewel   in
its   forehead,   the   myth
of   desire   being   satisfied,
o   calm   calm   leaf
of   nothing   &   all–

(untitled)

The word *saudades* cannot easily be translated. Our mother & i translate Brazilian poetry, & when we come to the word *saudades* we hesitate. Sometimes we write "longing" or "homesickness" or just *saudades*. "Estou com saudades" seems to be a condition you can have in the very presence of the longed-for object, an emotion that is also a philosophical condition, that grants possible time to come into alignment with impossible attainment. Proust, of course, knew *saudades*. Our mother tells a story of going back to Brazil in the 1940s for a visit, after she is engaged to be married to our father. In my mind she stands on the deck of a ship with several languages in her brain, holding her notebooks. As the sea knows time, her words know air. Her imagination is full because she is young, & she is not a bit lonely, just as a word is not lonely. She looks into the great black waves of the Atlantic. When i ask her about her childhood in Brazil, she begins: "On the day of my birth, there was a small revolution, so we fled into the countryside." Humans have that ability to collapse realities into manageable units: "What did the streets of Porto Alegre look like?" "They were stone, big granite pieces, horizontal on one side." (*paralelepípidos*.) She looks over the edge of the ship. She has a precise interior world; she has a body like a poem, fragile but strong, orderly & unknowable, very capable of doing things. Soon she will see her own mother. There is no one like her, there never has been, there is no one like another person. The visible stands for everything, including the invisible. The great spirits visit. World War II is over. Dark waves slap the side of the ship. There now. Let's begin our life, *com saudades*, looking for what is here.

for HFH

A palavra "saudades" não é fácil de traduzir. Nossa mãe e eu traduzimos poesia brasileira e quando chegamos à palavra "saudades," hesitamos. Muitas vezes, dizemos "longing" ou "homesickness" ou simplesmente "saudades." "Estou com saudades" parece ser uma condição em que você tem a presença real do objeto muito desejado, uma emoção que também é uma condição filosófica, que concede camadas de tempo que se alinham com a realização impossível. Proust, claro, conhecia isso com exatidão. Nossa mãe conta a história de voltar ao Brasil na década de 40 depois de ter se comprometido em noivado com o nosso pai. Na minha mente, ela está no convés de um navio com vários idiomas em sua cabeça, segurando uns cadernos. Assim como o oceano conhece o tempo, suas palavras conhecem o ar. Sua imaginação está cheia porque ela é jovem e ela não está nem um pouco solitária, na mesma forma que uma palavra nunca está solitária. Ela olha para as grandes ondas negras. Quando eu faço perguntas sobre sua infância no Brasil, ela começa: "No dia do meu nascimento, houve uma pequena revoluçãvo, então, fugimos para o interior." As pessoas têm essa capacidade de comprimir realidades em unidades manejáveis: "Como eram as ruas de Porto Alegre?" "Elas eram de grandes pedaços de granito, de pedra, horizontais de um lado" (paralelepípidos). Ela olha para além da beirada do navio. Tem um mundo interno preciso; tem o corpo como de um poema, frágil, mas forte, ordenado e desconhecido, muito capaz de fazer as coisas. Logo verá a sua mãe. Não há ninguém como ela, nunca houve, não há pessoa alguma igual à outra. O visível vale para tudo, inclusive para o invisível. Os grandes espíritos visitam. A Segunda Guerra acabou. Ondas escuras batem do lado do navio. Ali e agora. Vamos começar a nossa vida, com saudades, procurando o que está aqui.

para HFH

Curl of Hair in a Drawer

(a revision)

Writers long for a new sense of form though they may never know
what it is. The real is released from its concept, light releases day
as a fawn steps over the floor of the world till some of the spots
look spilled . . .   ⸬   In the 80s

    i traveled to see Plath's stuff like a pilgrim tracking relics
of a martyr. Some aesthetic camps didn't like her – too much
emotion or too much motherhood & in those days writers stuck to
their camps, though it seems like great writers abandon their
camps & are burning the maps to stay warm . . .

A librarian brought the drawer of Plath's things: satin baby book her
mother made, bits of a cloth dog & a curl of hair in cellophane [◎]. The
    curl befriended its zeroes. The penetrating light was huge but
    intimate.   Light pressures human monuments from
    outside, a pollen-colored cast to it, particulate but weighty,
as a girl felt trapped & insufficient yet possessed of deep & vagrant joy.
Hair is odd, more active when saved.   i stared at it a while;

---

    i was a few years older than Plath when she died; we had things
in common: mothers who made baby books; small children;
depression in the overwhelm; perfectionism. i love to write
more than i love sorrow. i love humans more than death.
    The somehow is endless, the details are endless & language is

endless so i lived. What would she have made of her fame, of poets only
read a little then: Niedecker & Hurston, Forrest-Thomson & Guest.
As a fawn steps over its dots, what we love keeps us alive. Sometimes.
Some of us. Mostly alive. In a curl of the mind from a curl in the mind on
the floor ~~xxxx~~ of the world, the unplanned monuments of light survive—

The Family Sells the Family Gun

a prose ballad

i only held it once but thought about it often as you think about those times when your life had stood both loaded & unloaded

One brother knew of its existence having seen it where it languished in the famed green storage unit from which it had been transferred to the bank-box but we never quite knew when

Information our father had & something he was squeamish about or proud of at the same time the way Protestants are about genitals

We believed it was a Luger–maybe taken from a soldier–in the War our father trained for but didn't ever get to because he was wounded in the knee–"sustained" is the word they use–sustained a wound–in infantry maneuvers before his men were mostly killed after D-Day–

When his ashes in the desert grave were lying we took the weapon from the bank-box

i put it quickly in my handbag to get it past the teller–the holster was the smoothest leather–brown & heavy –the yawning L-shape of the Luger Google says Georg Luger designed in 1898 –the holster smooth as the jackets of German soldiers in the movies & what had they done to make the cowhide smooth like that & what had they done to the cow

We thought of burying it in the desert but if you Google *burying a firearm* it
    changes to a search for *buying a firearm*

You can also look up how to load a semi-automatic weapon on YouTube
    where a white man with thick hands & a wedding band shows you how
    to check for rounds in what order & tells you how to handle it with your
    dominant hand

We couldn't take it to the cops even in my handbag though Arizona is open
    carry & you can take it anywhere in public but the cops can shoot you if
    you take your gun to their station

One young Tucson cop named Matt agreed to come to us & checked the
    magazine & said it was unloaded– looked upon us with excruciatingly
    mild pity – said this relic might be worth some money & stroked it the
    way some boys do

i couldn't tell what the brothers were thinking– it felt like a tragedy but re-
    versible – our father's ghost stood like a tall working summer like Ham-
    let's father's ghost appearing only in the day & good naturedly telling
    people not do the killing but still trying to control the actions of the
    play

You can think about ghostly word weapons nonstop   *Let's just take a shot*
   at it   *She was going great guns*   *He loved her but couldn't quite pull the trigger*
   Better to just bite the bullet   *Kill an hour or two*

& for some reason maybe sorrow for our father's power/lack of power i felt
   a twinge when my brother whisked the tiny heavy out of there –my life
   had stood a secret little hiddenly shameful semi-automatic firearm &
   When at night Our good day done i guard my Master's head

My younger brother sold it for $600 at a Tucson gun shop – one of those
   outfits where the master paces behind the counter offering advice on
   collecting & is so proud of his stash

It was a Tuesday i think–a Tuesday inside history where America is lost –
   & what should we do with the cash

for my brothers

Describing Tattoos to a Cop

(after Ed Sanders)

We'd been squatting   near the worms
    of the White House lawn, protesting
the Keystone pipeline =$=$=$=$=$=$=>>;
    i could sense   the dear worms
  through the grillwork fence,
    twists & coils of flexi-script, remaking
the soil   by resisting it . . .
        After the ride in the police van
    telling jokes, our ziplocked handcuffs
pretty tight,
        when the presiding officer asked:
    — Do you have any tattoos?
    —Yes, officer, i have two.
    —What are they?
    —Well i have a black heart on my inner thigh &
        an alchemical sign on my ankle.
    —Please spell that?
    —Alchemical. A-L-C-H-E-M-I-C-A-L
    —What is that?
    —It's basically a moon, a lily, a star & a flame.
He started printing in the little square

MOON, LILY, STAR

Young white guy, seemed scared. One blurry
    tattoo on his inner wrist i should have asked

what his was but couldn't
cross the chasm.   Outside, Ash
Wednesday in our nation's capital.   Dead
grass, spring trees
about to burst, two officers
beside the newish van.   Inside,
alchemical notes for the next time–

Chicago Black Friday Protest Near Apple

My grandson Cole & i stood outside
the Apple store in Chicago with
    chanters & dancers protesting Laquan
        McDonald's murder when cops
began to kettle, a term for making
        a danger circle that always sounds
like crayfish are being boiled alive . . .

            It's Black Friday according to
            retailers. There are maybe 25 protesters,
all but 3 are black; there are 16 cops, all but one are white.
        We could taste fire in my mouths. Apple employees
            had locked themselves inside but we were using
iPhones so cAppletalism is still winning. The tenses are shifting
in this scene. . . .
                    These are my children
            says the grandmother   in A Good Man is
            Hard to Find, but one cop has hatred in his
            eyes while the other cops try to look natural.

        Cole is 16, i needed to get him out of there & it's awful
        that being white we can.
            Over our heads according to theosophy
the Buddhic body the astral body & the 3-fold spirit world . . .

        The changes are taking too fucking long.
        We're tired of this. The goddess Astarte has
        fire in her elderly skirts. It's best to try no hitting first.
                But each minute has a separate brain
            & if the cops start to hit, i'm no longer
                sure what i'll do—

Crypto-animist Introvert Activism

a haibun

Every week for about a decade some of us at school have been standing at lunch hour to protest drones, racism, state killing, the death of species & so on. We stand under a live oak while people walk by on their way to lunch. We hold up the signs. It's an absurd situation & it changes nothing.

Sometimes the good doctor Ali brings a boom box with Bob Marley & we dance ineptly on the pavement. The changes fall together. Positive & negative fall together as Bob Marley sustains us near the tree. Cesar Vallejo dances as a flea on the back of a squirrel. Blake & Baraka dance as lithophilic microbes inside the rock. We have no proof that they don't. The science moths dance in the live oak & go about their work of being powdery. The protest is absurd but i admire these forms of absurdity. When the revolution comes, the polite white mothers in the Moraga Safeway will still be shopping for sugary cereals & barbecue sauce. When the time comes, some will rise & some will dance & some will lay our bodies down.

Triple Moments of Light & Industry

During our protest at the refineries, our friend R tells us there are bugs in the oil in the earth-colored vats at Valero & Shell, tiny slave bacteria changing sulfides, ammonia, hydrocarbons & phenol into levels of toxin the mixture can tolerate, & then we consider how early tired stars gave way to carbon molecules a short time after the start of time & now carbon makes its way in all life as the present tense makes its way in poetry, the sludge in the vats where the hydrocarbonoclastic bacteria break things down to unending necessities

                   of   which Dante writes

                         of   the middle of hell

               light   where no light is–

R says his friend who tends the bugs for the company feels tenderly toward his mini-sludge-eaters, they are his animals, he takes their temperature & stirs them & so on. We pause to think of it. Such small creatures. At the beginning of life the cells were anaerobic, ocean vents of fire, archaea, then they loved air. In the axis of time there are triple moments when you look back, forward or in. As a child you were asked to perform more than you could manage. Your need was not symmetrical. It is impossible to repay the laborers who work so hard. R describes his friend's work as devotional. The bacteria do not experience hurt or the void but their service is uneven & that is why i protest.

To a Life Ended in Winter

After our hearts were broken
could we love the little lights
    in the trees   faithful
in the dimensions
        as seed followers
pressed   on spiraled wires
    along the avenue
        to night   where you
also cramped the light
    with fringes & shadows
    your mind
that never will

        Odd friend
        ring-bearer
at the wedding of opposites

    the glowing tablet holds
your sentences in part
past the violent election
a violent not
        red ocean

    the us that is not you
        has such blunt company
    the you that is not
you past memory is art

for WG (1959–2016)

Hearing La Bohème after the March

on the plane from D.C. loaded with old
protesters   Oh wait that's me   My row all white people
though the plane is not   The middle seat woman   holds a crumbly
bent paperback   plus a pencil for underlining   Lost her phone
at the rally   Afraid they'll crack her pass code   The window seat
woman offers condolences   Calmly & nervously   they process
the march   i put in my earbuds   sleep over Ohio   i've been
a little tired since 1969   Darkly & singingly   warm storm clouds
parallel   Angels of a third altitude   drift amazingly by

In the headset *La Bohème*   the first half mainly   poor artists
Si mi chiamino Mimi   Mimi by the window   Mimi with her sewing
losing her key   then Rodolfo helps her   but can't save her
Mimi choking   from TB bacillus   Trump would stop
her health care   Paris 1830s very little coal   the July revolution
happened   It will happen again   Puccini composing late
in the century   Affairs with singers   & a cousin of his wife's
maid   When he was a poor student   he pawned his stuff

Art stretches out   over the abyss   Warmish clouds stretch out
Too warm   The clouds are hurting   Not Alternative Fact
i hear my seatmates talking   through the earbuds   saying the left
should get unified   i'm not that into unity   i tithe
my rage   It's absolute on certain days   Unmedicated moody
rage   Thursdays & Fridays   What i need is sleep   though
i love their tones of voices   the curious   strained secret
& querulous tone   the furious resentful   the held-in
the lovely   & sometimes say nothing   grandmotherly tone

There's an endearing light fuzz on their faces right now   They liked
the more positive speeches   not Madonna blowing up the White
   House   Mimi sings bravely then Musetta   Oh my beauties
   My other car is Ezra Pound   Profit is president   Not just this
clown   It's dams in Uganda   It's poppies for Percocet   Thumbs
   of the five-year-old   blowing up bridges   while his dad shops
   at Walmart   Thinks God is a Redskin   Use the bathroom
you're born with   The dad thinks recycling is a government plot

Art stretches out   over the abyss   Musetta's waltz stretches out
   interruptedly   *Quando m'en vo'*   Some artists fuse their Mimi
& their Musetta   those crushed by circumstance & expressive erotic
   flirts   Musetta knows her beauty   distracts one lover with
the other   i was marching for my mother   For six friends with
   cancer   for JR's hurt hip   SO's hurt hip   BF's hurt hip
texted some signs   till they cut off the internet   WHAT WOULD
JESUS GRAB   Luminous day   Smushed brown black white bodies
Yes some complained   Complaints are also music & the breath

   Was marching with my brother   & a half a million others
   Marching for our father   who loved democracy & opera   Sure
knew his Puccini   *Che gelida manina*   He held our mother's cold
   little hand   i'm crying at Musetta   her sappy gorgeous high
notes   The vowels drop with wings & mood   The angel of third
   altitude drifts up   from spooky inland   One seatmate spills
her water   We pass the napkins over   The other frets about
   the pass code   Sister it's too late   they have broken in

The cloud has a wound   The state has a wound   It guards
the wound with violence   We resist & then we know   Bodies
go with politics   Sex goes with politics   Art isn't politics
    Can go beside it though   A radical hope   lives on in us
i fear the short   attention span of the left   & middle left
self-satisfied recaps   We create & then we know   Some stepped
    on the little bushes   in the Capitol gardens   cared for by
workers who may not vote   Gardens where my love had walked
Golden trumpets will appear   maybe will   just not quite yet

    i don't fear death   i fear a future without art   The state
        vascillates   Simpering & thug idiocies   The bacteria in
Mimi's body anarchically spread   Is bacteria plural   Her song
distributes color   It's not that hard to love who you already love
    Broken songs are not for rallies   They're to keep nearby
while you prepare   to act without results   Angels of third
    altitude in the pre-above   holding used paperbacks drop
seeds of love & rage   or maybe   seeds of rage & love

    What is a fact   Most angels are not real   We continue
    in the chaos   The coulds & zeroes   The shadow banks place
ashes in the snow   The ashes bloom from coal   & promises
    So it was that our capital   seemed like Paris for a time
So it was that avenues bloomed in spokes for a time   So it was
we had each other   Aiiii!   My foot hurts   It's the left one
The day was pretty magical   That's not a lie   There's energy
    in some complaining   One laughs & sings about her shoe
        The other sings her name   so it won't die

for SM & BBH

Near the Rim of the Ideal

My anarchist & i   fly home   from the east
in sight of the rim   of the ideal   — —;
                                        on the right
    the least moon drops   — — a vitamin
b,   simple, pink, mechanical . . .
ellipses on the wing   in seamless   patches . . . . . .
    nails by Boeing–
        this week,   the horror   in Gaza,   in Ukraine,
            a plane shot down — — the concept of *nation*
stalls   in the bitter brain (bitter brain bitter brain
bitter brain . . .)

We've been asked to think   about Jefferson   – uh–ohoh
    founding fathers   — — the founding
            words search for their roots
        in air — — *federal*   [*"Why are you making*
such a big
            federal case over it . . ."] *federal* from *bheidh,*
                    meaning: faithful;   *fiancé*
        also comes from this
                What are we faithful to?   love's   mystery
    at the rim   of the ideal color between
    shapes . . . Monticello's columns   are faithful
        to the porch — —   they look like:

        @ @ @ @   @ @ @ @
        really do   really do

        really do   really do

        really do   really do

& the copula– – not stopped   by beauty or distress–
          Doric – –   enlightened thought,
     faithful   to space,
  & space   is faithful to the circular – –

          Deists liked their God   absent & elegant
          . . . . independent God,   a rationalist –
where   is He hiding?   maybe that's little Him   near
          the wing, floating,   neutral
  in   neutral mist,
          far from Jefferson's house – – now,   why
                         did he think he deserved all that?
          slave houses & smoke houses,
              the dustless silks,   the clock   he designed
              with his mind, with his mind   – –
  patrician rocking chair   called for by   natural law . . .

          My anarchist & i, we could love such a law
       as long as it's   the law of the rock & dirt   not
          my country 'tis of trading   metals & cloth
                    carried on the backs of children – –
              not   mastery over   persons
          bog turtle & purple bean,
       pale mucket, & sneeze weed,   *nnnot* mastery over vetch,
              mastery over independence   as in
          we sold these truths   to be self-evident as in
              Mileage Plus from Chase, zero percent intro annual
                    fee for the first year
       then $95 after that
       not mastery   because skies are friendly,   mastery
          over water because the slide   inflates automatically– –

my anarchist & i declare   dependence
         on the invisible,
                 & on its runt   the visible . . .
         not to hold   these truths   to be self- evident
if specifics fail . . .
Now far   far down   in Jefferson's garden – – in
rungs   & rungs of fixed   dirt   the united snakes &
         embryonic   spirits   push breath
                 into   pollen puffs   above
         finely ridged   carrots & onions ɪ/ɪ/ɪ/ɪ/ɪ/ɪ/ɪ/ɪ
                 connecting the ideal   through their roots   – –
pushing miraculous periscopes   out of earth,
past the fungal layer   of powdery nonDeist   soil,
         quite   dependent spirits all over the place   – –
we hear   he tended it himself . . .
                 O Jefferson,   paradox,   finest of men
         who wound down like his clock . . . . Slaves

remained & he was neutral as god
& he was neutral as god
he was neutral as god
was neutral as god
neutral as god
as god

                 We,   the difficult   daughters
         hold these truths   to be   selflessly   evident
                 as   microbes on   our nationless eyelids
         await   the arrival of the sun–

III.
Metaphor
& Simile

24 journal poems at year's end

I've never known such a springtime or experienced one to such an full extent as the one last year . . . Maybe that's because it came after a year in a prison cell or because at that time I had an exact knowledge of every bush and every blade of grass . . .
> **Róża Luxemburg,** letter to Hans Diefenbach, March 1917

I just didn't feel like obeying his demand . . . I was quite tired after spending a full day working.
> **Rosa Parks**

Lichens live on sunlight, air and water.
> **Stephen Sharnoff,** *A Field Guide to Califoria Lichens*

A feel, a sentiment with its own interiority, there on skin, soul no longer inside but there for all to hear, for all to move.
> **Stefano Harney & Fred Moten,** *The Undercommons*

for **Robin Clarke, Tongo Eisen-Martin, David Lau, Frances Richard, giovanni singleton,** & **Jessie Sandoval.**

Day 1

A metaphor appeared,
a form of action, while we were reading
just below the trees. It made
a human & nonhuman meaning. . . .
(not sure what nonhuman meaning means)
So, here we are now.   Unknowing beauty among
the brutal days. All year they sat out
reading, each to the other, in their skins. Days

	of	drought in the west,
written	of.	Writers
are stressed most	of	the time, trying
with many forms	of	life to make energy among.
Dry months	of	people reading, greenshield
lichen reading		to the fence. Indicator
species. Indicators	of	health, in the twilight
	of	a terrible year, *crepuscular*–
a Stevens word. Acts	of	gather & burn (what now
is called	*the*	*undercommons*). Rosa Parks &
Róża Luxemburg,	the	violence they endured
amid	the	infinite failures, unbearable
if you read	the	histories. To keep a little
hope but how:	the	young. Not to drown while
trying to register	the	forms of suffering beyond
or in	the	*the*, as Stevens wrote,
the mixture of	the	dump. To love, despite
collapse,	the	life forms
reading to	the	wood . . . frayed ends of

```
days. Days in        the      mind. Wood mind. Science
also reading to      the      dream–
      ,  , , ,   , ,  , , , , ,
      ~~~~~~~~~~~~~~~~~~~~
===================== (log)
```

Some people think lichen looks dead but it is alive in its
dismantling. Some call it moss. It doesn't matter what you call
it. Anything so radical & ordinary stands for something.

Day 2

A simile sets up space   for you to doubt
ever getting past the suffering . . . Rilke
Wer, wenn ich schriee, hörte mich denn staying mostly
in his room   & where if they cried out,
Who, if i cried out could hear the children killed . . .
A figure of destruction came to us & said,
such admirable life forms on the street as if love
grew black threads . . . To be with friends
you finally see, inside a grief year,
class grief, race grief, loss of love & rain. Ruffle lichen
spreading near the lake like similes.
(~i~ had not checked my phone . . .)
We need to talk. Wood mind. It's not just about your
own little darling, the wife of the decomposers said . . .
Remember summer the poets
read aloud inside their skin *where the undead meet the dead*
Voices sliced across the dusk, black cilia,
                              to   read to each other
in beauty in the dusk.   to   see black-edged
life forms on fences   to   lean against
                                              ovals of energy
while people said listen in the modest dusk,
                              to   register the horror
                  then   to   pass energy across.
Cortex K+ yellow, medulla K-, KC+ red to orange,
looks like punctuation while growing along, knowing
almost nothing, there are twin
sides to everything & the beautiful
wrong side is always listening . . .

Day 3

A metaphor exists in your place.
　　　　Thinking of Róża & Rosa
　　　　　on the tiny plane flying over Ferguson,
　　　the Midwest generalizing bumpy clouds,
iPad, iNausea, iVomit, a white woman throwing up in seat
9A into the paper bag.　A metaphor exists in motion.
　　　No one could help her as she vomited, we all just sat
there, helpless. My wife of decomposers has brown skin,
　　　she visits me among the forms. Lichen says
accept what is then break it down.
　　　~i~ sought my soul
　　　among the books & he was reading . . .　In summers,
beside,　they abide,　　they　　sit in yards & rooms,
listening to words,　　　they　　smoke hand-rolled
　　　　　　　　　　　　　　　　organic weeds,

　　wildly gesturing,　　they　　take the grief
　　smoke into　　　　　their　　bodies–
　　　The revolution it isn't coming very fast.

They breathe.　Here
are the durable goods online,　our phones made by slaves.
　　our satchels made of soft cow. During the *Can't stand it,*

how to live: skin in the yards,
      life forms, species on stucco & bark,
    lobes on fences like old sentences, shield
  & speckled, breaking down progress, breaking down hulls
of ships at port near tiny foxes in the woods passing through
    the organisms breaking things down,
Flavopunctelia in the lacerated dusk, o world/s that are &
     aren't, that is & isn't a metaphor–

Day 4

,   In the afternoon of our unknowing
,   we were outside. So were
,   other organisms: flies, dust,
,   punctuation. It's impossible to know
,   how to live: Rilke paralyzed, depressed
, wrote little during WWI. Claude McKay, Jamaican
      songs in dialect. In letters, Róża writes:
  my gold . . . The workers strike. The tsar's children had
diamonds sewn into their clothes. My lichen figure
.   has orange skin, she breaks things down in thickets

      near the walls, sunburst form with
    even oranger ears . . . living bravely when
.   the air is bad . . . yes of course, yes. Walmart
. doing violence to the poor who work & shop
    at Walmart how now brown cow
they cannot live. Dream baby. Crowds were
.   in   the streets
    again   in   groups. We had a brief
  window to join   in: black + brown +white
  students, middle in-   come adults, whatever
  that means,   in   our case teachers with

                jobs. No rich   in   the streets, no angry
x   Lloyd Blankfein   from Goldman Sachs
x   in   the streets after
x   poor people lose housing, how can he even look
                at himself   in   a window. Who if they
x   cried out. Now   in   oaks nearby, secret
x   life is growing, life forms, *Xanthomendoza*
x   growing real gold radar ears. A simile
                grows like the skin of the soul
x   if it were safe to grow outside & live . . .

Day 5

The metaphor for justice came to us & said—   *
what. What did it say. It was hard,   *
   & then a tone or pressing   *
rose inside the mind &   *
 doubled it, undocumented love came back   *
(~we~ had not checked our phone . . .)
The end of racism not near, banks with
  new toys selling triple debt & greed—
      no end of fury over this
   the end of our undoing cannot see . . .
   in brief grief woods, the many colors
  like a 12-toned scale of . . . Life destroyed
in undertow, detached . . . the secret figure came to us
  & said, someday, a people & post-people.
Those who still had energy blocked the road.
Some got mad over this, sure. Red Róża's
letters overwhelmed
             by   suffering,
             by   news of killed workers,
overwhelmed   by   children,
             by   human cruelty, holding
a gun to get her pamphlet printed . . .
    My wife of decomposers
has tubes on her skin, a metaphor for getting
        by. A calm

life,  *Hypnogymnia*
tubes & big ears listening in thin woods,
an undercommons in the tree–

Day 6

In the aftermath of the overwhelm
~we~ hope to stay awake. Oxalis tries
to stay awake, living in the smalls. Friends,
when you were low as children, which punctuation
did you love. It tried *to, to, to, too too too* help you along,
as lichen reads the stone, as Rosa rides the bus, as
Róża rides the train (Microsoft doesn't want
to paste the Polish ż in Garamond & they say
Bill Gates has 36 bedrooms)... Róża looking
at the sky out the jail cell, vision released,///::: To human
suffer so far back beside... outside the drought,

ruffle lichen spreads	a	tasty dark beneath a tree,
white lobes with	a	larger lobe & soredia looking
like ridges of cocaine		when we were bored & didn't
know oblivion is	a	nother thing Big Pharma
owns...	A	simile besides. As
	a	child ~i~ thought ~i~ could
love everyone	&	now ~i~ can't. Can't

love George Zimmerman, Darren Wilson, Netanyahu. Tech
support tells me she hopes this app will give our family

	a	*new found freedom.* ~i~ am
	a	twin, the other voices

are invisible. Algae & fungi, twinned,

"with lobes 6.2- mm wide	&	long cilia" "fairly common
on bark in the cortex K	+	yellow, medulla PD-, K–,

to escape the nothing. ~i~ love it when young poets
read outside bringing 20 styles of natural into line. My
brothers' train set had   a   clump of plastic lichen

representing *nature,*   a   world that dreams beside

as when   a   poet reads

outside within   a   dappled afternoon, her

voice like someone   leaving Eden in a syntax

of three smalls, no binaries,   no false praise or bullshit–

Day 7

A metaphor returns with dots
of otherness– this is not that. Disperse the self,
serenity & grief. Serenity of Rosa P. How did she
manage that. When ~i~ pray to the ground
the wife of the decomposers has bronze skin
& so does Mary Magdalene . . .
Solstice approaches, huge
patches of firedot species cover granite
outcroppings "opportunistically"–
at school   for the die-in
students go in   &   shout, don't shoot,
drop down   &   stay down, you & ~i~
                 &   we; the action
lasts about 4 minutes on the cafeteria floor, looking up,
lovely old brass chandeliers my love saw as a child, now
black students, brown students, white students,
some staff & some faculty lie there in
angles of below. To think of mothers of killed boys,
to have your boy shot in the back. Can't know, to
show up for an action in despair–
not to feel good about "being supportive."

To be & be below & feel.
The silence lasts 4 minutes, it has bronze skin . . .

Then students went back outside to the unknown. *Caloplaca*
clinging to its sunlit rock. You can't remove a crustose
species from its substrate without wrecking it,
who if I cried out. ~We~ need a different angel, firedot
species clinging to a sunlit spot of next . . .

Day 8

      ~~a simile makes oval meaning
to the side. In the hills,
    Pertusaria amara around a trunk of
drought-struggling laurel, intensity °°°°°°
& turbulence apart from this, bitter wart lichen
      that tastes like aspirin if you lick it
on your finger, *one must have a mind–*
bittersweet as humans have their experience,
– love & justice, the two layers with
   experience deepening the transfer. Róża L.
    & Rosa P.   Lichens are calmer than people
  & similes calmer than that.
Stevens writes *behold* (such an angel word)
as a listener – Toomer writes *in their hip pockets*
as a thing that's done . . . Róża's body floating in
the Landwehr –unidentified for a while. Meaning gathers
    in the doublesunder . . . ~i~ made that word up.

                You   can never
tell what will come out   of your head
    in the drought   you   sit outdoors
    with poets,   you   could be
      any of the poets of history, suffering beside, as
a simile, broken & not,   as all people   are helpless

     & notice & suffer . . .

Day 9

           The cops seem younger
than our undergraduates. Their very arbitrary
  boundaries make no sense. Some must cross
      over to continue being human . . .
Across the invisible, we hear the great dead
   purring at the back of history's throat,
    as people report being called to heaven . . .
Rosa & Róża move there freely, & Amiri,
  his heaven next to the street the astral plane
has solid sounds & when ~i~ die
~i'll~ whisper some to you . . . There's a species
of *Cladonia* called British soldiers, –grows sideways
     on old stumps–mini-muskets
      in the mist, "fruiting bodies" with minuscule
crimson hats . . . ~i~ used to have more sympathy for cops–

mostly working class,
idealistic– but now ~i~ don't.
   Out in the dark, a few desultory
old white teachers, the untired kids & anarchists–
     ~i~ flap my stubby wings. Farewell
    to Florida. Protesters have a right
to lie down, to decompose, to be a form of life, to die
   or pretend to die beside other forms–

Day 10

F & ~i~ look for lichen near
the train tracks, we make theories,
finding a couple of species that could live
together like justice & love, a
    Candelariella (gold speck)
    species that looks like burned-
    out undocumented huts from
    an invasion of yellow, –~~in time–
—blown out! (It is 1905
    in the *Letters*, Róża has
assumed a name, travels to Warsaw,
    calls her lover Leo "Gold"–
        down the street, someone holds
            a FUCK CAPITALISM sign
        beside the scraggly Santa . . . shoppers pass by . . .
Our other species for today is a 1963 mod-yellow-
comes-off-on-your-finger species *Chrysothryx*–
we decide it sounds like the witch in *The Tempest*–
        F checks her phone–
Sycorax–mother of Caliban (*this thing of darkness
    I acknowledge mine . . .*)

********+++++++

Day 11

The job of a soul is to stay awake;
the soul is a metaphor. In my metaphor for metaphor
~i~ hope to stay awake. Here at year's end the ring
        of   the eye of the kinglet precedes
one   of   its colors. Usnea clumps in
some   of   the dry oaks & the fox enters
              the rimmed burrow ... in the human
sphere of   this disaster, billionaire
humans throwing money at the fracking lobby ...
My wife of decomposers has sage skin, she will
not purr unless the air is good & says you're not
  in a dark mood you're depressed–
      Stop, mighty city spread out– much of life–
to be beyond–O Capital our Capital our fearful
      ship is done ... beside the Bay,
the one ~we~ call Much Beard hangs upon its
      central cords, sage green, proud, manic,

avuncular ...
      in   a day, can't imagine Róża sleeping
      in   jail, circles intersecting,
      in   love & justice,

"now prison stands before me or I before it," writing
    of demonstrators gunned down before
    the Winter Palace ... (can't fathom having energy
for her good cheer not knowing how if you saw
    children beaten you would not hit back–)

Day 12

     For fifty years my figures have appeared . . . the figure
of destruction comes in many forms & lately she wears veils that
look like netting or hashtags,   *Ramalina*– a Kali figure of
change & destruction. When ~i~ was a girl upon a desert hill
she said you're more than you, love comes & goes– Do
you want me to say ~i~ don't believe the spirits literally?
~i~ believe them more than ~i~ believe California Penal Code
Section 835a, & when ~i~ asked her recently she did not say:

*Any peace officer who has reasonable cause to believe that the person to be
arrested has committed a public offense may use reasonable force to effect
an arrest, to prevent escape or to overcome resistance.* She did not say:

*A peace officer who makes or attempts to make an arrest need not retreat
or desist from his efforts by reason of the resistance of the person being
arrested; nor shall such officer be deemed the aggressor or lose his right
of self defense by the use of reasonable force to effect or to prevent escape
or to overcome resistance.*

The wife of decomposers did not say that.

Day 13

Some say poets should not use metaphor . . .
oh–sleepy leaves, who did not understand– some say
you do not *use* it,   everything is *already*

        it,   & thus

        it   is our heart, which is a

metaphor & not. It   was a dappled afternoon,
no binaries, no   false praise or bullshit;

        it   was apparent something
                had been transferred &

remained untraceable.   What is poetry for?

        Its   lives become untraceable,
                the faster magic of

        its   skin comes back, all

the raw power   you had. For poets

        it   is an undercommons,

Fred & Stefano   note: skin, emotion,

        it   registers as life forms ~~~

Lecanora with   its   creamy apothecia growing
like baby epics   on a branch & this is what

        it   will be like in what we

want to call   the stateless world, & when

we dream   it   stays with us,

                  it   stays with us,

                  it   stays for all who

                sit   in the dusk with poetry

loving the world. . . .

Day 14

A simile sets up gaps for you
to doubt when there is disagreement
during 525,600 minutes in a year & news
    outlets tried to focus on kids
breaking windows without focusing on the profit,

that it stays
        with   them, sick profit stays
        with   them, profit stays
        with   their families like sick
skin   with   their personal islands' skin.
Justice & love like back & forth. In 1909 Róża
    summons the Black Forest where her love has been . . .
in jail, she longs for the gray badger,
stork & weasel–slick along the ash & larch, tucked
among them there. Imagining the next life of
Monsanto CEO where he has to
    search for bits of metals in toxic waste dumps
after all the suffering he has made–
now that's not nice, main brenda. The afterlife is
    a simile & not.

F & ~i~ discussed feeling approaching
form in Walter Benjamin, a mystical union
where you feel something approaching always just
outside the forest
of modernism trying to get in–
**************>>>>>>>>

Day 15

A metaphor might make more trouble
when it tries to be . . . the grief of history . . .
not a gold as in a Rothko painting,
middle gold despair . . . Rosa riding the bus,
what rim of light she saw
in that brief-as-a-pine-tree moment past
concrete sending the growth out. The young
strike back for what has not been struck
enough in striking hours by the marginal–
When ~i~ think of our students
~i~ feel less despair. That they grow. Tendril,
glome, lobe, *Rhizocarpum geographicum,*
cortex UV orange, medulla
K-, KC-, C-, P+ yellow or P-, maps rising
on Sierra hills as far as snow can't see, spreading,
& the black bear lumbering by to her cub,
eating garbage in drought-driven

flurries, almost solstice . . . M mails a picture of lichen
in the snow, how will it survive
i wonder . . . Róża writes in 1916
"They sent candy" & talks to mice in jail as she's trying

to figure out the uprising . . . working at
   the everyday, in our need to feel less terrible,
      in their need to be loved,
      in your need to be loved for what
         you are but cannot be—

Day 16

This spread out life form, like a feeling
on a tree . . . simile . . . fables of love, "relationships,"
the toxic metals tick inside our phones . . .
The beauty   &   symbolic peril
                     &   the shock of art so
weak some days . . .   outside, sunlight spreads
over winter mice   &   down to microbes
of eternity–   &   then returns
to a changed   world . . . People cluster by
their phones,   anticipating news, some
are setting fires &   who can blame them . . .
soil listens to you,   soil listens in, the soil
of the beyond   where some rise up
                   &   some shall sow
                   &   some shall sew a thing

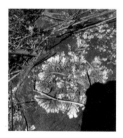

so true to the invisible
& some strike out
    &   some refuse. You go out
in your neighborhood, it's dusk, drought-
ridden browns & peaks of thistles not post-
anything, the world's body like your own,
not one that is & isn't you–

Day 17

      ——too tired to drive yet able to bear stress
         while moving like all the rocks south of Cascadia–
            Late sun rock slanty slanty forms late
          sunlight slanty slanty forms dead deer by
        the side of the road &   wings of the new
bridge   ~~   ~i~ lost my way & don't know how to live
        ~~   Put the phone down, not s'posed to text now
        ~~   Someone has to keep watch
        ~~   No use to fling anxiety out there
        ~~   Wish they had an app for how to live
        ~~   Apps are corporate crap watch the road
                 Creeley sd
        ~~   Too tired to protest anyway
        ~~   You're wasting energy with your anxious thing
        ~~   ~i'm~ not not not not not not not
        ~~   You're s'posed to sleep at night
        ~~   No ~i'm~ not shut up shut up
        ~~   Nothing is being helped by sleeping less
        ~~   ~i~ know why Baudelaire smoked so much
                hash while trying to work the barricades
      Not to despair yet to look out, to somehow chant
profound & blare each molecule existing here in
      circles at its will, something will outlast
      the scene, anthropocene, ~i~ write to you near
Xanthoparmelia here, "perhaps the most common
species" on granite, nameless energy
      till all of life seemed wrapped in it~

Day 18

> ~solstice approaches–a summary of itself–of
> pure light–a guild of poets through the year
(retrieving what Stevens called the late plural),
> to be beside, like a simile, to keep
my white ears open, to study the undercommons,
> as they said . . .~this journal
> precluding certain sounds even
via other pronouns. The wife of decomposers
> appeared with white soredia & said
– i call upon the wiser ones ahead
– they want to keep their guns & who can
> blame them they're sick of it
–i see the cities someday, people having food &
> work they like
–& certain people dead
–you haven't slept enough not up to you

> till black *Nephroma* breaks things down
–a little rain coming in they say
– millions of humans in their need
> in their need to eat & be loved in their need to
> eat before they are loved before they're
> loved a little for what they are–

Day 19

       Was hoping to stay awake & not to hate . . .
Had——what. Honestly? Nothing. Sorting nothing
    out about the murder of black children,
  months of loss & violence The figure said,
 a miracle still found here, double, hope &
      grief, dark active freedom running on the fence
      elusive & remade, what
  can we know about experience. A man
showed F & me how to slice *Everna* lobes across
the medulla–

              it seemed like feeling sliced open,
all the layers there, then ~i~ was hopeful for the humans . . .
     Today young juncos
       searching for wet seed,
   one day relief from drought, next day, drought,

to show respect	for	wedges of their solidarity
black hoodies	for	brief loud dowsing units
of rain,	for	mid-December sharp wedges
of black	for	conjuring Berlin where
Róża is writing	for	her workers page by page,
wedge of black	for	not doing nothing, tired

thought   for   tired young workers, Robin in
  Pittsburgh,   for   Jessie in Ferguson, David
    in Aptos,   for   the ideal past the peril
     of the time. . . . Black hoods of juncos in
    the oak we stand below, *Flavopunctelia* undercommons,
cortex K-, KC+gold, C-, P- medulla K-, KC+pink, C-, P+
red orange, one of our common species as if justice
    & love were one & lived outside the heart
in the eye of the cloud plus here
    in my pencil unowned by any system–

Day 20

The lining of the real is infinite & that
      is where we live, & humans
   don't give up when dreams are momentarily
sundered . . . like Gogol's overcoat, like hope,
   the cloth of that transforming everything–
     ~i~ mean, the lining of that dream . . .
   This morning juncos with black wedges, black
hoodies in the nervous dawn . . .
     Solstice approaches, the children
  arrive at the end of an awful year,
grandmothers peek at them in their beds,
     there, not so terrible now, there they are
  beside the winter dusk . . . pale pink lights
lift in the malls, humans trying to make
    the living wage, in their loved
& unloved skins, brown, black,
   pink, beige, white, marked, scarred, inked
pierced skins, buying objects from each other
. . . desert children doubt the winter holidays.
My childhood Jesus lived inside a cactus, magic
  liquid streaming from his hands– the soul as
causeless love. On winter hills, bands of scrubby
sunburst lichen eating lignan in the mist,
a beetle, the cells of its vision over gold,
    its labor not labor if it doesn't think so

nor *Xanthoria*   break-
ing things down, "fairly common on bark . . ."
if you peel a piece of it from history
the rest continues–

Day 21

        The wife of decomposers came to me
past fear. She very said, she very said, when they rise
      up they will rise up it will
take decades when they have to . . .

	It	was the longest night,
	it	looked like much
continuance,	it	wasn't clear; had seen
a tiny one on a sidewalk		spread in a rosette

distinguished by	its	cortex, a love supreme
in Coltrane,	it	looked like *Sit there*
in the air,	it	looked like socialism
after money . . .	it	was night, my love

had gotten up perhaps to read Colm Toíbín or
Hamlet commentaries, ~i~'d gotten up to pray
to moonlight, to water & dark energy & wordseeds,
to spirits of dead children, to sorrow circles around
    mothers of killed children,
mothers of babies lying in the straw, in the dirt,
 at dawn read Red Róża's letters from the jail, not
solstice fare exactly, *My good spirits don't hold up*
      against my yearning . . . She imagines a trip

with a baby beside her, speeding along, it is spring . . .
  The child & ~i~ played on the rug,
    games of war & recovery, giant bugs, dinosaurs,
      we played You will return to magic
though your parents' marriage failed,
      we played The day was ravaged into streams
but everyone was saved . . . though in my head it said
        with the grown-up voice *& thy*
rivers will only guess the place of thy rest—

Day 22

Oakmoss lichen *Everna* was used to preserve wigs.
We took the family to the singalong Messiah.
The conductor wore a fake Handel wig. The child had
watched violent cartoons all day while we bought time
for cooking Christmas dinner. Róża writes in 1916:
"To be a human being is the main thing above all else
... to joyfully toss your entire life 'on the giant scales
of fate' if it must be so ..." ~i~ forget every wisdom
during the holidays ... *Every valley,* the families sang
off key, *shall be exalted,* first performed for the poor in
debtors' prison 1742, ~i~ thought of musicians under-
neath their itchy wigs with body lice in 1742, an oratorio
about suffering, Jesus who invented the thing of
don't hit back, so few believe it now, thanking Jesus
at the country music awards by night & wearing
hats with gun insignias by day, even some poets thinking
AK 15s are cool, students tired of *don't hit back*
what with racist cops & tanks being rolled in & most
people think some killing in advance might work
if used correctly, some cite WWII, most think there are
some types who must be put away, insurgents bankers
immigrants settlers anarchists cops terrorists capitalists
rebels rightists communists bombists imperialists
abortionists nationalists breeders people from the east
& after that our side will remain. Out in the cold
    every valley shall be exalted while reindeer lichen
        sprouts from its powdery sides with no
           system of elimination or malice,

an indicator species, *Everna* with appealing
white on one side, green on the other, far
to the left in the winter night, breaking down
the fir trees & the human slabs & the little spruces ||_

(for MK)

Day 23

The decomposing wife rests in my trance
stateless state & metaphor tries not to despair;
the semester winds down, the usual
    holiday virus finds a host
    in bodies fed by sugars & salts &
delicious bourbon & slices of orange . . .
    carols from old northern forests,
        it   was   a dark forest,
    each bell   was   plagued by nothingness,
      ringing   was   brought along by doubt
& magic; ~i~   was   taking the child
    outside to see ruffled double things along
the ground, we were beside the spirit world in this
        mild winter, Žižek (Microsoft won't let me
paste v's on his Garamond Z's–)
      says we're not supposed to get "comfort"
from "nature" & ~i~ don't exactly

                                        but love how
leaves & wood & lobes distribute everything,
    a cinnamon revolt, the spirits
bringing a less grief-stricken day,

the bumpy undercommon thing
if you just walk along with a child looking
at mute colors not giving up–spice or dramatic
ochre or a soft after, even where
the dream is momentarily sundered~~

****

****

===============(log)
~~~~~~~~~~~~~~~~~~ (undercommons)

Day 24

The feeling is the lining of the dream.
             Each   day as a making &
  unmaking,   each   person loving & failing,
the hope   each   day that having to live
 in this dim   country will seem better
at some point &   each   body of each person
  will have a right . . .   The little boy & ~i~
walked with our lichen bag; he out-walked
    the sadness of his parents, ~i~ out-walked
    the facts . . . Feeling basically all right
is a privilege few can afford. Our neighborhood so
 full of plastic crap on Xmas eve, lights up
in early dusk . . . but there's an appealing multiglow.
Trace in the mind, Pound said . . .
    & always the counter-thought, the dialectical
    paradox in each event, history unfolding, –
the neighbors had put out their tacky 50s crèche,
    donkeys & sheep, plaster baby Jesus in
the plaster manger . . . Look at this, Baba,
  Leon said, standing a long time

with his bag of lichen,
unrejected & beside.   Maybe the child Jesus
    just felt electrical like Whitman did,

pushing what light he had out of his hands,
maybe ordinary light, we just don't know . . .
Man of constant sorrow. There are no reports
of him laughing, except in gnostic texts.
Murdered by the State for loving criminals.
Where did he get the idea. *Is & as* . . .
the world in all its forms—

IV.
Two
Elegies

The Rosewood Clauses

(for my father, Jimmye Hillman, 1923–2015)

*I dreamed my father was dying. He said he wanted to
arrange exactly what corner to meet him in heaven. i told him
heaven didn't have corners. He said his did.*

i.

Meaning is history but how is meaning made, was the thing
    we wanted to know.

i walked with my father for half a century on Tucson
streets near their house. We walked up Fourth Street
    & then cut over to Rosewood–a rectangle
        that shrank as he aged.

We talked about the *meaning of life* as if the phrase
    could touch the original flame.

A cashmere thrasher flies over the mint moon,
    gives off a little string of errors & there was
      meaning outside meaning where animals lived . . .

    our father's cane had nerves at the end of it.
   Nerves & nevers. The cane's exclamations points
  tapped down Fourth Street where
baby palm trees like Tucson sports hair
    rose from concrete with
     gnats on salty stilts to greet the clouds
  above the summer harpist in the sky;

had left my reading to walk with him; had left my room
    where i had fallen in love with literature–

ii.

The visible is thick but it can always be
got through. Charged particles enter the earth.
     Everything is active, just in time . . .
We talk to the clouds: cumulus, cirrus with
  the feathers–

     Cacti of all ilk. White
     gravel in Tucson driveways,
     wrought iron on windows try-
    ing to look Spanish, adobe houses.
   On painted mailboxes, folks started
putting things like poodle icons, saguaros
made of knitted wrought iron & Ford
Thunderbirds being ridden by cherubs
with smiley faces; he didn't notice
the mailboxes but knew almost each house's
history up to Craycroft. i love barrel cacti, they are
    specific to the oddness of the living,
curly spikes & waxy peel-proof fruit

with hooks (????????)
no space between blossoms when they
thought themselves up. The heat swelled so you
don't notice climate change. At 13 i got rid
of hell, but there is a crinkle in the soul as it
adjusts to the heat.

You strike a word & a group comes back–
whether in this form or not, we cannot say–
there's a crinkle as each word adjusts
to the heat–

iii.

i've studied the soul, know that it exists,
know it is a construct & an animal mist.
He read existentialist philosophy in the sixties;
      thus he quoted Camus & Sartre to his children.
Never gave up on Christianity, the Jehovah kind,
though he liked Jesus just fine. Left home at 15, sent money
back to the farm. Hurt his knee in WWII– in infantry practice
not combat–before most of his men were killed.
It bothered him as we walked. What is the meaning
of experience, was probably
what he meant. Meaning is a glimmer; it leaks from the words.
He wanted to be a writer & writers struggle with this,
      some imitate others who have figured out meaning &
      few are given credit for what they do, they crave a little
      credit but it rarely comes so they go on
    writing then become the mists of history. The mists can talk.
           That is what i mean by the soul. Our father was
a cheerful person, a bit pompous which was sometimes funny. . . .
Liked to make pronouncements about "mankind." (Mankind
is what accompanies daughters.)   Here we are in 1965
before church; my cousin Gloria texted me this. Papa
is about 42. i look like I'm 42 but I'm actually 14.

iv.

            Blue molecules have flame
         tusks when they recede into desert
ground. The ants take these for labor.   Tucson
       greasewood bushes thrust forth
            permission pom-pom frenzy clumps
      near the remodeled homes. Imagining was actual.
     i could see his faults but nothing 2 decades
    of therapy couldn't fix (my therapy not his :)
       Under awnings, on adobe porches
tiny dogs yipping . . . the annoyed white
people in shorts, yelling at the dogs insincerely (the passionate
hope your creature will be nicer than you are).
    What is the meaning of so much heat. The yards are still
mostly neat in their neighborhood,

     even where heat-bald gravel driveways
grab the fastfood wrappers. The future has three shoes, &
  that moment between me & my father lasted 50 years.
There is a layer of meaning so vast it can't be borne.
You see between clouds from the airplane when you
     leave Tucson, silhouettes of clauses when the
    flight attendant asks what you want to drink, if you cry

you want to be comforted & the plane flies through
delivery systems of air, over strato-cumulus between now
& Los Angeles. All beauty has
         meaning even in your pain. Western suburbs are
      spreading out, eating the species, till
   all galaxies will have our cogs & chips & oil & drier lint . . .
Being a daughter prepared me for literature. i had left my first
loves to walk with him: my mother, my brothers, the spirits,
my library books with their glamorous silences of immensity . . .

V.

The Rosewood clauses are the reality of childhood expanding &
   contracting their error.
          Slow down, greasewood. Slow down cumulonimbus
      approaching from the west. i'll talk to you later. We are
   on loan from the miracle. Wrought iron held the American flags.
                  Our father was a happy person. Why?
   Basically, certain brain receptors,
      plus, there is a zone of joy. i don't know where. Carry on,

   dusty concept—
      there was his zone of joy
          where the sting of poverty was gone & hell would
             go to hell. The family, the human family,
          had meaning. Why? Put it this way: i have no idea.
   For me it is symbolic & literary like a group of energies
             each holding the unknown. He liked numbers when
   they rose. He felt joy & sang in church.   Tap tap went
      the cane, & Tucson beetles past the wooly stalks still
             gather in the lower shapes of air. Arizona ants
             pull seeds into the red dirt home,

into the physics, cunningly, listeners,

a piece at a time, dragged to the whole. Watching Tucson

ants is like teaching the ode to freshmen. Good job!

Walking the same neighborhood as walking with P

in the 60s, *Larrea tridentata*. We talk to the clouds.

Ovals then continuous

doves pierced them constantly, from the stone habit of the Catalinas.

Life is but a dream; our father loved that sort of bromide.

Carry on, dusty concept, lacy white attachments where

the needle emerges from the flesh of the cholla, stay with us, dusty

gravel, the xxx you can't tell anyone, & the sleek rabbit turns

its moist eye & enters the ground

where everything gathers after humans are gone–

vi.

The visible is thick but the invisible is thicker. There,
meaning searches for itself. There, the soul moves
   without wings, through vague altostratus.
When he lost his temper, not even
            the lizard found it &
stones talked at the edge of pride–;
         the small rabbit runs under the thrasher.
   If you are a daughter you long for approval

& being dutiful is found in literature. P up the street
in his house reads also . . . It's 100 at 6 p.m.
Desert roaches scuttle–their antennae recognize
         an odd woman's thought & they
         will send signals when we die through
         storms & rising heat. He was an economist,
         when we talked he gave advice about money
         which i ignored . . .
      i couldn't convince him of the horror of capitalism;

he was raised in poverty & loved new shoes.
Around us, the pronouns,
    the loud midges & fronds, singing without spending,
    the active souls are communists with dust motives
& sprinkle their bounty around till we are left roaming.

vii.

There is a goodness that leads to nothing.
When our father lost his temper, not even
the thrasher found it. Carbon the avant-garde of growing
  & the uncharged particles entered the earth
from elsewhere to rest in our
neighborhood– in the rectangle of
               meaning, the life of being in families, carbon
                       with its allotropes
                  coal & diamond, 4
                 electrons, its diamonds &
                speed, hexagonal darkness
             with electronegativity, thank
          you Wikicommons, with its radius,
        with its mercury mouth, thank you Bob
           Dylan, with its atomic number 6,
            thank you Rincon High School
              1968, carbon speeding
              along as we walked
through our brief life together. In his nineties, he put
his shorts on over his pajamas. As here–the picture's

kind of blurry. Past mesquite with
considerable thorns & disturbance of yellow. i whisper to the lizard
before my father sees. Mr. Lizard with your
travel math, you mean everything to me,
everything is not the opposite of nothing–

viii.

My father left home at 15
& sent money back to the farm
he left home at 15 & sent extra money back to the farm
tried to do his duty ~~xxxxx~~ uh uh uh uh huh huh
    trying to finish the blues–
rhymes with farm;   harm   storm (thank you Sterling
    Brown, Bessie Smith. Thank you Bob Hass.)
Form rhymes with farm.
      His people are buried in south Mississippi but
his ashes are in the desert ground.
His folks are buried in south Mississippi but
his own ashes are in western ground.
He was a cheerful person, nice to be around. Mostly.
                      He was
                 a cheerful person.
              Why? Well, smart big
            friendly handsome white
          guy in the 20th century who
        talked a lot. Women loved him. Not
      all women. Most men loved him; &
    once when he was 91 he said to his helper,
  "Fred? I don't think much about the
afterlife, this life is pretty damn good. I'm
sure something exists besides myself, but not
much! Ha ha, write that one down, Brenda!"

ix.

i've studied the soul. i know it lacks wings– or rather,
   the wings are sort of a cross between a dove, a metaphor &
     the invisible. A little shout out to George Herbert here
       with these wing shapes. The meaning of meaning floats out
       of the invisible– a somewhat
        tautological situation. . . .
              Up Fourth
           Street, past the closed
          up houses. Tucson more
         than doubled in the 1950s
        Great climate for half
       the year, then heat only a few
      can love. Climate change, money,
     in small pieces they have not ruined
    earth. Down south, the haze
   of the copper mines. There is a
  leaking out of everything. The ants
 work underground; the invisible
is a communist. For ants, meaning is a
a few molecules their sensors pass along,
taking their crops underground. Some farm
aphids. Our father who art in Agriculture.
A ladder of clouds. Summer thunderstorm
  gathering. Reality is thick but can always
  be got through. The middle class was folding
  in the mild suburban neighborhood, a century

of capital. Mr. Lizard
with your silver studs, you enchant our family
with your brine horizon . . . i will be old now just
    in time to laugh with him. In the clouds,
his laughter is general now, believe me.

X.

It is hard to mourn a happy person who did not fear death
but there are things i can tell him now that he's everything.

Half life of the soul, carbon in the nothings where
nothing is pointless, flexible nothings & the extra
   energy in matter, all elements, the neighborhood where
each plant has a timing–sage o'clock, half past creosote–
   whether in this form or not, we cannot say,
Under puffy alto-cumulus, hairlike cirrus.
He loved humans but could be full of
     judgments his children & his friends put up with,
     but mostly the indomitable search for–what?
Don't be so certain, calcium
     clouds, it's not the same him existing past the fake
     owl on the neighbor's antennae, the straw in palm
     fruit rustles & the thrasher– curved loud beak–
He thought that meaning matters but
he never hurt anyone with that belief,
     unlike Bush saying Jesus told him to invade Iraq.
     My father was a practical person; meaning had a
physical aspect as if leaking air through a faulty gasket
     between the worlds.

xi.

Toward the end of the walk his shoes make
galaxy medallions & a slight squeak
as we neared the house where Mama prepared the snack.
                    Tucson ants assemble
                collective meaning working
                together & each carries a
            combo seed past the Ford Mus-
            tangs, counting seeds like Psyche
            in Ovid & Duncan, it is up to us
            to keep her changes going in
        new poems. The spirits are thirsty
    in Tucson, they have time, unlike God
    with his famous schedule who allowed us
    to invent him
after the lizard
made itself. When i
go inside the earth,
there are sections. In consciousness you get to
save sections but not the whole thing.

xii.

The invisible is thick. In the middle layers
    the living get by . . . The why seeps to the side.
      You will always miss your father, listeners.
        Venus, Regulus (i hold up my sky app)
a voice among the great dead hath let fall
the Rosewood clauses.   Dim in the desert
   the tortoise carries its firm squares on its
   back, green into gray;
      here's sage for you, & ragweed.
Color is my favorite & clings to my skin
whether in this form or not i cannot say,
      The lid doesn't fit between worlds
& our father leaks back through. Tucson heat
is absurd but i love it. At dusk the confused
roaches come out in the streets.
We are almost at the house. Bring your ants,
      sleek cloud brocade of science
      speaker, bring your galleries of rain–
When they ask how
they will know you, i will tell them–

Her Presence Will Live beyond Progress

(for C. D. Wright, 1949–2016)

She was here

Her presence was most of it

     She made each day
                    by responding
so there was   less agony among us

She preferred words
    as action   not contingency

& one time when we went up a khaki hill   out of necessity
her face turned red above the kerchief
      in the west   laughing
          part of a previous

      & the earth was either caring or not caring
      we don't know which

She was born   She made each day
    by responding

She was the funny one
No one was all that funny compared to her

Her brother said she went to law school for a while

She was here
She had everything about her
She was independent but related
     & that's what she wanted

She made the days
     by responding

She had hair like a fast pony
Thick   not well-behaved
     Might be called a pelt

Her brain said   among other things
     caint for can't

Take that time

     (–I waddn't any saint

You were a kind of saint   caint saint)

Even the blue eyes had an accent

The osprey passes to the west
Its undecided underwings the color of alder bark

In the ecotone of the beyond her face is light
      as what's next
            three geographies   & one flame

In the ecotone of the beyond where we reach her in the hills
      That whole thing of wearing

     —

     —   floating fabrics

    —   — —

The fabrics floating by on bodies of women

floating by   beside the violent fact

The young want to speak of what's next in poetry

i ask her fabric spirit where it floats

& hear   nothing for days

Fact & the myth of fact

What's next is what could not
         not be here had poetry
         not been here
She knew that

The rocks turn under the earth
Half her face is a map of the other continents

That whole thing of   we are gathered in the desert

The sand smells like the present tense

      She is worried about sand
          in the sandstorm   sand
              in her hair where you can't even
          see your own hand

& she says   Let's just put our shirts on our heads
          Dudden matter
              & the rocks turn under the earth
        The jewels turn under Africa

She shouts   as she rides the dumb beast

In the crater of no names she has a name
In the mountain of cries   tiny glittering reptiles

& one time when she was supposed to be positive & say
    nice things at the conference she said
I caint teach like that   I'm mean as a snake

In the ecotone of the beyond   she is funny as hell

What moves in the mind?
    The spirit world   as valley wind?
A full memory riding with shining scales
A friend moves in the mind

Where are you

    —Goin around the bend   of the cave

How do you spell your middle name

    —Starts with one of the curved letters   Maybe a D

Have you heard about the new planet

—I like the old planet just fine   Rising   Falling   Hovering

What is the rest of you   past this impossible   sorrow

—You decide   You're the one who believes all that stuff

She lived completely in the countries where she went
She danced in the galleries of countries with prisoners

& one time in Africa she put fabric on her head & passed
              the flask
      of the short prisoner under the table

Where are they now
The revolutionary guard   The friendly assassin
              who was proud of his jacket
      the poets jailed for 1000 years

& between each thing   between every soul on earth
              the million golden   stitches of fate
      threads sewn   by women
threads sewn by   the women & the slaves

When people ask why we need poetry
they know
they know what it is

We don't read recipes at the graves
We don't read tracts & theories at the graves

The little countries turn in the sand   sand-sound bleating
      & the death of each woman
              is the death of a century

Where are you now?   which news is true?
i open your sisterly books

(What are you working on

      –I got a lot of it done

"What's next in poetry"

      – I just want to poke holes in their egos
           sprinkle out   the one big self

What is "what's next" where you are

      –They don't have that much next around here

Do they have a you right next to the us

–You decide   you're the one who believes all that stuff)

She was born
She creatured   & repeated

The cloth made by inventors of cloth who have no name
rode among them
      on the dumb beasts
      on the crotchety beasts
where the sound of the grass in the caves barely covered
      the oil   the thieves had come for

Riding along in the dunes laughing about the camel's bad breath

The fabric under which
      she rode still exists
        & the dumb beast past the bombs of militias

& all the dirt that rests in the caves of the arches

& the fabric goes by on their skin   like what's next in poetry

      Civilization   costs you extra

Up north we talked about the big quake   we'll float out
        on California
      start a fresh island just for readers   & babies

(Look at those ash feathers
              drifting from the trance candle)

& one time we got up north
      after the conference   after the good cheer
          of the parrot

She lay down in the warm ash   dripping steam
        of the geyser
                & said   —Oh man!

The black stalks of vineyards   twisted
          like restraint   in excess

Talked till late   two "high strung" women
      in the wet black ash

Talked about guilt   fear of stupidity   the unjust
          ugliness   & the banal
      fear of not loving   what you love   enough

  The judgment of our Southern fathers
              who started out   real smart & real poor

In the valley of waters
sounds like the updrift of
        her personality has been sprinkled around

Downy woodpecker   pounds from the middle
    of the live oak   near valley vineyards
        near the geyser

Something trying to do something effortful & unlikely

Some of her energy   up through blue curves of the geyser
People trying   even harder with their kids

        —who knows if any of that
    will work out honestly

Abide a little bit   abide abide   sister colorful
you don't have to send messages yet

& she appears tracking lines under my pencil

(—see if you can find me)
        the joke has an accent

            (—didden it didden it)

two oak leaves at the bottom of the mineral pool

i can't be a good Buddhist
near the Buddha pond

    i cling to her like a burr on a sock
   cling to her like a lipstick stain
cling like lichen on the live oak   breaking things down

   extra hidden life   among the years

She had the beautiful   unusual
    face   pretty much
      like a field hawk
         Hopkins' kestrel
her prey   was pure sound
    caught this morning morning's minion
     rising falling hovering

& one time   we talked about
      the difference between prose
         & poetry (life or more life)
Words she loved   how they break down & stay

As trees everywhere have two things
     cellulose & lignin

& the fabrics go by on top of the women
     in California as in Africa
     the perfect inventors who have no name

(Where are you being everything now?

−sort of particular speckles all around

Where are you going in the hidden mountain
     home

   −oh just floating around poking holes in people's
     egos)

Let's be realistic she wrote

We're never coming back

She was just trying to be sassy
She knew   we never know

(What seems to be the problem i ask her
            into the emptiness

–I can't buckle my fucking invisibility suit)

Examples   disagree   with eternity

& one time when we were in the desert
    with our beautiful men
        we saw the Bedouin women

    selling baskets   sand blew in our faces

We talked to them

        lots of smiling

We understood nothing

Each time you do something good
        it is the only time

            so you love it unbearably

& for Forrest Gander
January 2016–January 2017

V.
Two
Odes

i must be careful about such things as these.
Ed Roberson

Poem for a National Forest

—And the wood spoke, as paper.
—What did it say?
—Well, it said "What did it say?"

a.

The goldenrod bent as they passed.

Asteraceae.   Stars in that.   Syllables bent
   in what they said to each other,   crab spider
changing to join.   It had been
a terrible year
              but only the humans knew–

Now a little pleasure
        in a place "set aside" –aside of whom, set by what–

the couple walked & the syllables paused,
      yellow cones clumped
                 in the tops of white firs *Abies concolor*
      tight mini-masters of the zeroes . . .

Great blue ones waited,   immortals waited
   & the punctuation   of John Muir.
         "God cannot save them
from fools,"   he wrote.   The couple paused
         Relax   implied the one.
         I can't   replied the other.

b.

There wasn't much she liked about the
nation, but the don't fuck it up & try harder
than usual in the national forests concept she
liked just fine. It was mostly white people in
station wagons till the 80s then mostly white
people in SUV's with dangly pine-smelling car
deodorizers bringing sad or happy children to
camp-grounds but after decades more people
of color & trans people came & it was less
lonely. Some people from the interior wanted
more hunting & motorized dirt bike trails in
national forests. The children played with
rocks then with video games in tents & their
fingers outnumbered cinquefoil & fleabane &
checker mallow & pennyroyal & horsemint &
tiger lily. People who had lost their jobs
gathered in tents & sealed their Pringles from
bears, people from other countries & large
families for 3 days celebrated birthdays, they
brought mute dreams into tents with beer &
shadows & flashlights in their phones, they
stared with awe into the pines, they lived in
the 12 natures & forgot how to die.

C.

John Muir friend of reality
strapped himself to a tree

> [Safari cannot open page because
> too many redirects occurred]

i've heard John Muir that lover
   of reality climbed a pine
         during a wind storm

[Safari cannot open page & Apple names
   its systems after big cats that have been
murdered on safaris like Cheetah, Puma,
Jaguar,
Panther, Snow Leopard; the cats get bigger
the more they are destroyed]

Muir's father beat him so he ran away & some
   might say he practically invented nature

The beetle would not say that

"what centuries have passed," he wrote to
         keep God separate from his father

"pines bending like grasses"
         "kingly sugar pine" "elastic temper"

d. *the writing between forest & mountains*

Unconscious spoons of ice scooped
up this valley, history
        was invented.   The Cathars
thought
                Lucifer fell smack
into the garden . . .
                & meanwhile, beetles
chew
the trees, meaning by erasure, prefixes,
syllables,
   inventing humped letters not in English
though, the engraver beetle, the wingless
ambusher,
        the elderberry beetle,
        & today i have fallen in love
        with the borers & the sawyers
        writing in the cones
        with larval forms of the obtuse

for they love wood as i love paper,
pressing
        their whole jeweled bodies
in the beauty of the bark, dark bark,
        sexy sexy sexy abstract beauty–

e.

A new baby has been brought
to one of the campgrounds.
   The white fir day-stills itself
     over the baby's cries, under

a massive cedar,	&	honestly the sizeable
blister rust	&	the shelf-fungi are
trying to rhyme	&	help the stressed
mother. Campers	&	day people don't
read much poetry		yet a few climbing
to the dark nipple		of Mt. Tallac might
read Basho	&	the meadow sun
	&	myrtle warbler both
hover over dots	of	*lecidia*'s million gray
black eyes	of	sightless quartz.

                    The forest waits past
any law. Be calm with me. Actually, you
   don't have to. The mothers
who packed lunches in non-recyclable

plastics relax	&	fathers relax about
having packed		too much stuff.
Brown fathers	&	black fathers,
white fathers	&	nonfathers try to
relax	&	John Muir
listens in heaven		if that is what you
choose.		If you do not choose
he listens		in this poem.

The tiny weasel sleeps under
the elevator stars. Don't look for me under
your bootsouls, look for us spinning multiply
with our poems   among elements
                    & our imitators–

f.

At their picnic the couple fed the ants
An older couple, they had loved for many years

Big Sierra ants climbed over vast twigs & even
      brought their dead to get to the picnic
      large of head & large of pine home
      They looked like *Camponotus* (genus)
      family *Formicidae Formicidae*
      (sounds so good because of miss-a-day)
      carpenter ants with their striped balloon
      thoraxes & their ballet type socialist legs

The older couple were both "co-dependent" type
      middle children feeding the big ants
      on purpose huge donations of sandwich

They watched whether ants would prefer lettuce
      or cheese or bread & the answer
      wasn't clear but one of the humans said
      this is about as happy as i can get

The air was light & delicious as mountain sex
The humans watched a while & kept climbing
The forest stayed calm for the next thousand years

though some of the species would never return

You who don't understand poetry
    Of course you do
    Stand in the shadows in a dream
    Write from where you are
    Write what you want to read

g.

They left disappointments to climb
The gray Here & the brown There
Existence gave up bitterness
& there were decades set aside
& the gold hopes of a twin
nothingness
in galleries of insect script

In tremble galleries the beetles wrote
They looked across the roots &
wrote
in galleries of spines & shards
Humans looked at the shadows &
the clods & forgot the terror
government

Each small section of the world is
owned
But meaning is not owned
& greed had not choked the lichen
or rock's first face of listening
Had not choked spirit & the wind

Human writer
Please don't start everything by
apologizing

Decomposition nearly caused you to
give up your staggering
under the maps
where you were vanguard only
to the night & the world
stepped lightly on the world

h.

History is passing in a series of Nike
ads   & Walmart still owns
the 18th century poor
You will have to stare at your cup of
staggering
The poor are armed in Texas
They are armed in forests to get
more elk   They bring their
        guns inside the theatre
They bring their guns inside the bars
& the lack of revolt is embarrassing
You stagger through the woods like
people in the Black Forest
        in the 18th century
like children at the beginning of this
book   You trade your grief for joy
& your heart hurts in the buckled
grasses
The arched & scalloped bats speed
out at dusk   & the fleas dance in
relief

i.

The trees went ////////// & they went
\\\\\\\\\\ They couldn't make up
Their minds YYYYYYYYYYYY
But the writing of the bugs & the humans
Was evidence that everything exists
The worse things went for the humans
The better things went for the bugs

The writing as evidence that everything exists
We wrote the names of bad legislators
We read them in front of their offices
You read them in the air & at the table
They will last for a while in your poem
But you can't write the names of species
Fast enough before they disappear

i will write the names when i get out of here
i will read the names of the ones who did ill
& the ones who did nothing
The colors are busy being themselves
They don't notice the public yellow &
The alpine green or the good we did
Between the thought of them

j.

Then it was that the jeweled beetles
                went back to the bark
To the writing of several statements
                without meaning
Thus it was that the meaning was
                made later
For there were 6 natures & they all
                could write
& the humans climbed past the
        sulfur flower & its invisible brother
Past seeds with their 2 million year
                inventions

Western molecules of day
                found prefixes
        on the bark & wrote
Though nothing would read them
We thought of our friend & there
                was her name
In the high altitude someone had
        carved CD i'm not kidding
There is a feat to being named
There is a feat to being always &
                being named

k. *(wood mind–for Anne Waldman)*

In the forests saved by good luck
something echoes the wood mind
A great being pressures the pine belt
   lying down in sessions of sweet
silent thought   i'm afraid some
     won't know Shakespeare wrote
     that not brenda
yes the bugs are a pest for human
     commerce
& yes the beetles write too loosely to
     be understood

   we walk past in the woodmind &
      wouldn't mind
for they are a fancy club of
     visionaries
the stag beetle the yellow pine
engraver before Urdu & Mandarin
the beetles write loosely in
     ampersands
past the triple sorrow curvature past
     air & script

& yes they are a pest for capitalism
they will probably rise anywhere to
anarchic things over tone

& lie down to rest in the forests
  in good luck beyond the mystery
& the jails   past the idea
even of the infinite
  in documents that
  crumble over stone

I.

Talking to other hikers we'll never see again

Stopping near mountain white thorn with
    juicy aphids all over

Maybe they are Mallarmé & Césaire & Ana
    Cristina Cesar

Mountain bluebird mother feeding its baby &
pine siskins eating
    pounds of bugs before tomorrow

This is our book of Days next we'll write
    hours & eons & time will be finished

Then despite everything there will be a quality
3/4 of the way between the pause & the anti-

pause in granite gilia where a little brood of
    siskins rests with the trumpets

It had been a terrible year but the air had
    made the brain   lighter in the skull

They looked for El Dorado the imperialists &
    it was hidden there

It's not that they could keep it

It's that the public climbed the mountain &
   didn't not feel joy

Poem for a National Seashore

The isle is full of noises,
Sounds and sweet airs that give delight and hurt now.
Sometimes a thousand twangling instruments
Will hum about mine ears, and sometimes voices.

Caliban in *The Tempest*, III.2. 130–133

i.

    –& humans walked to the edge of the sand
through a bank of verbena & fog;
    they thought they'd never get over
the deaths, but they were starting to. Worry
    about money rested in their phones. Talk of
candidates had stalled. Some sang. Grays of

    objects rested in their packs. They had come
to the edge with children or with friends. Big
    nothing quieted the crows. Wings of dried ink.
The snake had gone back to the hills, to velvet &
the brian-grasses; it digested a mouse near its spine.
    Some sang. The fox went back & would never

meet the snake except through the ampersand.
    The memory of failure failed for an hour. Some
    sang. The future was a cosmic particle
seen once a long time ago. Those who had tried
    too often walked with those who had yet to try
    as doubt can walk beside a radical hope–

ii.

some had cancer   some walked outside
    some were breaking up   a few

    were getting by   some walked past
pines   to their hearts' desire   thinking
    of sex   or seeds   a few   asked

    where nature is   bonnard-blue thistles

yarrow leaves   narrowly   out to sea

axio-fog of August   down from bluffs

    others rolled through   dune grass   some
rested   depressed   a few   made sand-

cities sandwiches   some went   birdward
    to sooty & long-billed   murrelet   grebe

iii.

–they had driven to the country, though as
   a poet wrote *The country will bring us no peace*;
they took their children of light & flesh
    because the sign was the sun upon the earth,
it was not toxic assets, it was not forwards or
   options or swaps; the sign was not ruin upon

the sea, for the sea saved some. A caterpillar of
   maybe it was the tiger moth inched along,
    a few white bristles sticking up, bristles taller
than the country, & *Abronia latifolia's* roots would
not live past the country or the blue-eyed darner
   & the meadow hawk with its three life stages . . .

By the sea the orbweaver rappelling beside
   the fleabane was bolder than the country,
    it didn't see underlying leverage or hedging,
didn't see collateralized debt obligations & rates,
   or see the probably 100 trillion traded on
what is called futures while the mountain lion that

has a small future took her young through the O in
October. Human children rolled through dune grasses,
   they had a simple laughter in the country, in sand
    so much older than the country, they had a little
gladness for that day while the sign, the shadow
   of death, passed over them but death did not–

iv.

little litter   on the littoral shore

where first peoples set tule boats

walkers   makers of a burn tangle

left that ocean   before writing nations

whose words   are lost   thick low

mats now named beachweed or heliotrope

horned sea rocket   When John Muir

a sweeping man settled farther inland

that family farmer   grew peach trees

o ever now   after such sorrow

we dreamed   a red ladder of

birth & death   being set down

V.

The sun paused. It was greeting the soul
of the day. The clouds gathered past money,
they were cumuli- & cirri-, they were glauc-
& grise & gray. The friends talked
with their thumbs on the tiny machines
& some walked or drank & some loved.

On the mountain in summer
they had seen serpentine & saw it again
today, black green not the color of money
as if a serpent had slid beneath the birth
of the sea & brought the burned
waves to the rock. The friends

had violence in them & they had
silence too. By the waves the silence
sounded like *swswswswsw* or _____,
it sounded like " " " " " " or even {{{{.
Lichen hung in hashtags & the wind
was braver than sports. Slowly they

forgot the grief opening of this book
& when they saw the secret serpentine
they knew what could be both you
& not you, that snake & fox &
word would live with the hooded,
the ring-necked, the marbled, the blue—

vi.

Otters swam in the lagoon,
the gates opened in the reeds,
no suffering between the myths or
silver smelt diminishing. No metal or
spilled oil where human hair had been
used to gather it . . . Otters have one million
little hairs per inch of skin so when
between the reeds they passed they did not

hurt with cold. Far out to sea 10,000 whales
swam without the humans.
The humans breathed when they saw them
not as dire. Liso- & lati- & beside. They stood
in *Abronia latifolia,* cries of *E* or *I* when they
saw the whales. Harbingers, Thoreau might
have said. One tall boy named Finn saw three.
There was aggression among large mammals

but no merrill lynching, no goldman saching,
no bankers' greed or quantitative easing
no negative interest rate environment
yielding minus zero so students pay to be
in debt. There was none of that. Some willow
buds bobbed in the lagoon, kelp bobbed
between gray & brown otters' heads in winter
cress. Their happiness was research.

vii.

The humans had come   in   strong boats
when continents   were closer.
That is the theory   in   some accounts.
The continents floated   in   & suddenly
naked-new bodies arrived   in   buckled dunes & radiating
grasses. When some made love   in   the wooden place
by the sea   in   autumn her hands were
always cold even   in   thick warm
fibers & out   in   the charismatic dusk,
under the harvest moon set   in   the history of
arrivals,   in   browns & gray of winter fog &
maybe   in   the amount of time
it took for the   in-   side of them to become
warm, jazz poured   in   as if from distant fires on
the west shore, as if   in   animated orange code.
Centuries
passed. When sex was delicious one woman thought, here we are
at a national seashore, almost nothing goes well for the nation
but land held in common past dominance & greed
which seemed like a real plan as if love were free

viii.

& heard the reeds hissing   when
Drake stepped on land   creeks went
below   the new dead in slim
fog could not be comforted

dusky *Chlorogalum pomeridianum*   the "soap plant"

blooms on dry hillsides   white-crowns nearby

cloudy light flowers   wiry blue lines

Miwok dug up   hidden bulbs   used

dye from leaves   for tattoos   used

raw bulbs   for lather   from cooked
bulbs made   a sweet starch   then

with the paste   they glued arrows

ix.

In spring, when the field starts to think & the invisibles
are relaxed, sounds let themselves out to the left. Crows
  & apples sanction their appeal & humans go out
    almost to the Point & see the baby elk that have
      have fuzzy fur on the horns, grasses through which other
grasses push. Yellow mustard flowers like paintings in
Europe. The elk are standing out at the precipice
    past dread or Thursdays & the humans start to feel

pleasure. Some humans don't want elk on their land
  & put up signs with poems: LET'S PROTECT /
BOTH ELK AND COW / TIME TO BUILD / ELK FENCES NOW.
Humans want to have sex anytime they want but don't want
  the elk to have sex anytime & accuse male elk of
    drinking water before sex, even humans who might
take property from humans in other countries think
male elk are being unreasonable for drinking water,

  but the humans love beauty & can be released from
their positions because so many have doubts about
  doubts about what is called the natural world; far below,
    the sea lions are stretched out like rug samples,
  & the humans tarry, looking down at high waves crashing,
  green with its leader into gray, crashing over what is lost;
the humans name what is lost while going home where
  they live in violence & hope & inconceivable longing–

X.

In woods where   the spirits stood

among the signs   past *usnea* hanging
in wet bishop pines   humans heard

the loud instances   of wide hawk

A red-tail   flew over them

E-E-E & the anti-going furred one
crawled past   brown feet of chanterelles

waited while one   of the hawk's

perfect E's flew   to the sky

& found the   end of time

xi.

They had come to the coast as they
   had come to songs as they had come
   to poetry. When they were odd
children they went to the sea & saw
  the bronze stems in the sand, dune grass
where the shaman starved & hurt sank
  quietly. The parents were anxious, so
the children tried to act normal to keep them

calm. They didn't know about threatened
   corals or the sorrow of coastal towns.
The children tried to act normal in school
    when teachers brought packets of poetry.
On holidays, violent games with the cousins
    & the sea grew more toxic &
more lovely. Now they are grown, they're
   trying to feel a little less terrible

about everything. They might take a poem
to the beach for a birthday or a wedding.
   Pelicans fly in their backward $\mathbb{Z}$s. Sand
is the residue of stars, edges echo eco
  eco, for the house is already beside itself,
    the edges not the center; the children
laugh as they make the sand houses, not
   remembering they'll remember –

xii.

So it was that the dream went back past the signs

So it was in summer again the loved ones went out to
    the sea at a quarter to dusk

The part of them that could do nothing did nothing
    & the light of them walked along

Walked west forgetting not the horror but forgiving
    others who were happier & the amount

When they got to the waves they gave the ashes of
    the dead to the sea oh blankness cut loose
    from the dream

& forgot for an hour the anger as they sat & shook
    the small stones from their shoes & walked
    back over the bridge of fireweed

Talking about events that mattered as the ashes were
    sucked back in the tide so loss could be lost
    for a while as love kept them
    in company beside –

for the children & grandchildren of the seashores

for Bob Hass

Acknowledgments & Notes

Thank you to editors of anthologies, journals & periodicals in which some of this work previously appeared: Academy of American Poets *Poem-a-Day* & *poets.org*; *Big Energy Poets*; *Blood Orange Review*; *The Boston Review*; *Bullets into Bells: Poets and Citizens Respond to Gun Violence in the U.S.*; *Cascadia Review*; *Colorado Review*; *Columbia: A Journal of Literature and Art*; *Community of Writers Review*; *Forum*; *Fourteen Hills*; *Ghost-fishing: An Anthology of Ecojustice Poetry*; *The Harvard Advocate*; *Harvard Review*; *HWAET!*; *Inverness Almanac*; *The Jung Journal*; *The Kenyon Review*; *Lampeter Review*; *Lana Turner*; *Lightning Strikes*; *Lumina*; *The Massachusetts Review*; *Monticello in Mind: 50 Contemporary Poems on Jefferson*; *New Yorker*; *Omniverse*; *Plume*; *Poetry Magazine*; *Point Reyes National Seashore Facebook site*; *Quiet Lightning*; *Resist Much, Obey Little*; *The Taos Review*; *Washington Square Review*; *White Stag*; *Wild Hope* & *Zocalo*. Thanks to Brian Teare who printed "Her Presence Will Live Beyond Progress" as a chapbook from Albion Books. Thank you as well to translators who have made some poems available in other languages: Hans Jürgen Balmes, Chen Li, Jeongrye Choi, Laura Contreras, Wayne de Fremery, Daniel Carr De Musio, Julia Fiedorczuk, Sebastião Macedo, Ricardo Freitas Filho, Jami Proctor, Xu, Zhou Zan, and Ezequiel Zaidenwerg.

Much gratitude is owed to Saint Mary's College for a research grant that enabled me to work on this book & to my colleagues & students at the College for their support & ideas, especially to Cathy Davalos, Chris Sindt & Matthew Zapruder. Bob Hass's *A Little Book on Form* provided formal inspiration. Thank you to the first readers of this book: Robert Hass, Angela Hume, Frances Lerner, Geoffrey G. O'Brien, & 'Annah Sobelman, & to everyone at Wesleyan University Press, especially my editor Suzannah Tamminen. Thank you to my family & friends for their love and patience.

The pieces in part 3 were initially recorded as journal entries, December 1–24, 2015. I am indebted to giovanni singleton & Robert Creeley for their daybook forms, as well as to Stefano Harney & Fred Moten, *The Undercommons*, Charles Altieri, *Wallace Stevens and the Demands of Modernity*, Róża Luxemburg's *Letters,* and to *Field Guide to California Lichens* by Stephen Sharnoff. Photos in the book were taken by me on an iPhone, or taken by passing strangers.

Brenda Hillman has published nine collections of poetry, all from Wesleyan University Press. Her most recent book, *Seasonal Works with Letters on Fire,* received the Griffin International Poetry Prize and was long-listed for the National Book Award. Hillman is also an editor, translator and activist for social, economic and environmental justice, and is a Chancellor for the Academy of American Poets. She serves as the Olivia C. Filippi Professor of Poetry at Saint Mary's College of California and lives in the San Francisco Bay Area with her husband, Robert Hass.